TEACHER'S PET PUBLICATIONS

LITPLAN TEACHER PACK
for
Dicey's Song
based on the book by
Cynthia Voigt

Written by
Mary B. Collins

© 1999 Teacher's Pet Publications
All Rights Reserved

This **LitPlan** for Cynthia Voigt's
Dicey's Song
has been brought to you by Teacher's Pet Publications, Inc.

Copyright Teacher's Pet Publications 1999

Only the student materials in this unit plan (such as worksheets, study questions, and tests) may be reproduced multiple times for use in the purchaser's classroom.

For any additional copyright questions,
contact Teacher's Pet Publications.

www.tpet.com

TABLE OF CONTENTS - *Dicey's Song*

Introduction	5
Unit Objectives	7
Reading Assignment Sheet	8
Unit Outline	9
Study Questions (Short Answer)	13
Quiz/Study Questions (Multiple Choice)	22
Pre-reading Vocabulary Worksheets	37
Lesson One (Introductory Lesson)	45
Nonfiction Assignment Sheet	47
Oral Reading Evaluation Form	49
Writing Assignment 1	51
Writing Assignment 2	54
Writing Assignment 3	61
Writing Evaluation Form	55
Vocabulary Review Activities	59
Extra Writing Assignments/Discussion ?s	57
Unit Review Activities	62
Unit Tests	65
Unit Resource Materials	99
Vocabulary Resource Materials	115

A FEW NOTES ABOUT THE AUTHOR
Cynthia Voigt

VOIGT, CYNTHIA (born 1942), U.S. author, born on February 25, 1942, in Boston, Mass. Voigt writes fiction for children and young adults. She has been praised for her strong characterizations and for her careful style of writing.

Voigt studied at Smith College, receiving a B. A. in 1963, and taught high school English in Maryland from 1965 to 1967. She taught at The Key School in Annapolis beginning in 1968 and was chairman of the English department from 1971 to 1979. From 1981 she taught part time and continued as department chairman. Her first novel, *Homecoming* (1981), was nominated for an American Book Award. Other novels included *Tell Me If the Lovers Are Losers* (1982), which told the story of several girls of widely different backgrounds who learn from one another as they form a volleyball team in college; *Dicey's Song* (1982), which won a Newbery Medal; and *The Calendar Papers* (1983). *Homecoming* and *Dicey's Song* tell of a young girl named Dicey and her siblings.

--Courtesy of Compton's Learning Company

INTRODUCTION - *Dicey's Song*

This unit has been designed to develop students' reading, writing, thinking, and language skills through exercises and activities related to *Dicey's Song* by Cynthia Voigt. It includes seventeen lessons, supported by extra resource materials.

The **introductory lesson** introduces students to the novel through a short discussion of moving and relocating. Following the introductory activity, students are given a transition to explain how the activity relates to the book they are about to read. Following the transition, students are given the materials they will be using during the unit. At the end of the lesson, students begin the pre-reading work for the first reading assignment.

The **reading assignments** are approximately thirty pages each; some are a little shorter while others are a little longer. Students have approximately 15 minutes of pre-reading work to do prior to each reading assignment. This pre-reading work involves reviewing the study questions for the assignment and doing some vocabulary work for 8 to 10 vocabulary words they will encounter in their reading.

The **study guide questions** are fact-based questions; students can find the answers to these questions right in the text. These questions come in two formats: short answer required or multiple choice. The best use of these materials is probably to use the short answer version of the questions as study guides for students (since answers will be more complete), and to use the multiple choice version for occasional quizzes. It might be a good idea to make transparencies of your answer keys for the overhead projector.

The **vocabulary work** is intended to enrich students' vocabularies as well as to aid in the students' understanding of the book. Prior to each reading assignment, students will complete a two-part worksheet for approximately 8 to 10 vocabulary words in the upcoming reading assignment. Part I focuses on students' use of general knowledge and contextual clues by giving the sentence in which the word appears in the text. Students are then to write down what they think the words mean based on the words' usage. Part II nails down the definitions of the words by giving students dictionary definitions of the words and having students match the words to the correct definitions based on the words' contextual usage. Students should then have an understanding of the words when they meet them in the text.

After each reading assignment, students will go back and formulate answers for the study guide questions. Discussion of these questions serves as a **review** of the most important events and ideas presented in the reading assignments.

After students complete reading the work, there is a **vocabulary review** lesson which pulls together all of the fragmented vocabulary lists for the reading assignments and gives students a review of all of the words they have studied.

Following the vocabulary review, a lesson is devoted to the **extra discussion questions/writing assignments**. These questions focus on interpretation, critical analysis and personal response, employing a variety of thinking skills and adding to the students' understanding of the novel.

There is a **group activity** in which students working in small groups to create "Dicey's Song," actual lyrics to a song that would be appropriate as Dicey's song.

There is a **unit project** in which students must *create* something. Many of the characters in the book actually *make* things; they are *do*ers. This project turns your students into *do*ers (for at least one assignment!) and gives them the opportunity to show off their own talents.

There are three **writing assignments** in this unit, each with the purpose of informing, persuading, or having students express personal opinions. The first assignment is to express personal opinions: students have the same assignment Dicey did for her essay--to write a composition about someone they know who has a conflict in his/her life. The second assignment is to inform: students write a composition in which they prepare for their **oral presentation** relating to their unit projects. The third assignment is to persuade: students are temporarily turned into marketing agents responsible for creating a full-page advertisement for *Dicey's Song* to be distributed by the book-of-the-month club.

In addition, there is a **nonfiction reading assignment**. Students are required to read a piece of nonfiction related in some way to *Dicey's Song*. After reading their nonfiction pieces, students will fill out a worksheet on which they answer questions regarding facts, interpretation, criticism, and personal opinions. Most students will complete this assignment in relation to their unit project.

The **review lesson** pulls together all of the aspects of the unit. The teacher is given four or five choices of activities or games to use which all serve the same basic function of reviewing all of the information presented in the unit.

The **unit test** comes in two formats: all multiple choice-matching-true/false or with a mixture of matching, short answer, multiple choice, and composition. As a convenience, two different tests for each format have been included.

There are additional **support materials** included with this unit. The **unit resource** section includes suggestions for an in-class library, crossword and word search puzzles related to the novel, and extra vocabulary worksheets. There is a list of **bulletin board ideas** which gives the teacher suggestions for bulletin boards to go along with this unit. In addition, there is a list of **extra class activities** the teacher could choose from to enhance the unit or as a substitution for an exercise the teacher might feel is inappropriate for his/her class. **Answer keys** are located directly after the **reproducible student materials** throughout the unit. The student materials may be reproduced for use in the teacher's classroom without infringement of copyrights.

UNIT OBJECTIVES - *Dicey's Song*

1. Through reading *Dicey's Song*, students will analyze characters and their situations to better understand the themes of the novel.

2. Students will demonstrate their understanding of the text on four levels: factual, interpretive, critical and personal.

3. Students will complete a creative project.

4. Students will be given the opportunity to practice reading aloud and silently to improve their skills in each area.

5. Students will answer questions to demonstrate their knowledge and understanding of the main events and characters in *Dicey's Song* as they relate to the author's theme development.

6. Students will enrich their vocabularies and improve their understanding of the novel through the vocabulary lessons prepared for use in conjunction with the novel.

7. The writing assignments in this unit are geared to several purposes:
   a. To have students demonstrate their abilities to inform, to persuade, or to express their own personal ideas
      Note: Students will demonstrate ability to write effectively to <u>inform</u> by developing and organizing facts to convey information. Students will demonstrate the ability to write effectively to <u>persuade</u> by selecting and organizing relevant information, establishing an argumentative purpose, and by designing an appropriate strategy for an identified audience. Students will demonstrate the ability to write effectively to <u>express personal ideas</u> by selecting a form and its appropriate elements.
   b. To check the students' reading comprehension
   c. To make students think about the ideas presented by the novel.
   d. To encourage logical thinking
   e. To provide an opportunity to practice good grammar and improve students' use of the English language.

8. Students will read aloud, report, and participate in large and small group discussions to improve their public speaking and personal interaction skills.

READING ASSIGNMENT SHEET - *Dicey's Song*

Date Assigned	Reading Assignments (Chapters)	Completion Date
	1-2	
	3-4	
	5-6	
	7-8	
	9-10	
	11-12	

UNIT OUTLINE - *Dicey's Song*

1	2	3	4	5
Introduction Project Assignment PV 1-2	Read 1-2 Orally	Study ?s 1-2 PVR 3-4	Quiz 3-4 PVR 5-6	Writing Assignment 1
6	**7**	**8**	**9**	**10**
Study ?s 5-6 PVR 7-8	Study ?s 7-8 Library PVR 9-10	Study ?s 9-10 Writing Assignment #2 Writing Conf.	PVR 11-12	Group Activity
11	**12**	**13**	**14**	**15**
Study ?s 11-12 Extra ?s	Vocabulary	Project Presentations	Project Presentations	Writing Assignment #3
16	**17**			
Review	Test			

Key: P = Preview Study Questions   V = Vocabulary Work   R = Read

STUDY GUIDE QUESTIONS

SHORT ANSWER STUDY GUIDE QUESTIONS - *Dicey's Song*

Chapters 1-2

1. Describe Dicey.
2. What does Dicey consider her "pot of gold"?
3. How does Dicey feel about school?
4. What did people say about Maybeth?
5. What was Gram's transportation to go downtown?
6. Name and give the ages of Dicey's brothers.
7. What does Dicey say Maybeth looks like?
8. From whom and how did Dicey get a job?
9. Where did Gram and the children live?
10. From whom was Maybeth's note, and what did it say?
11. Who was Dicey's English teacher?
12. Who did Dicey think was the only interesting girl in her class?
13. Who did Dicey meet after school?
14. How did Dicey and Wilhemina get acquainted?

Chapters 3-4

1. What important letter came in October?
2. Where was Dicey's old home?
3. What was Gram's response to the letter from Boston?
4. Why does Dicey feel that she doesn't have to worry about Sammy?
5. Who is Jeff?
6. Why does Millie always make mistakes on the order forms?
7. What was Maybeth's talent?
8. About whom does Dicey want to write her English composition?
9. How does Dicey feel about cousin Eunice?
10. What does Dicey first notice about Mr. Lingerle?
11. Why did Dicey almost protest when Gram asked Mr. Lingerle for dinner?
12. How did Dicey feel when everyone laughed at her home-ec apron?
13. What did Mina count on Dicey not to be?
14. How does Gram feel about getting welfare checks?
15. How did Gram respond to Dicey's question about the conferences?
16. How did James and the other children get into trouble with Gram?
17. Why did Gram and Dicey go to Salisbury?
18. What is Maybeth's problem in school?
19. How would Momma react to Maybeth's problem?

Dicey's Song Short Answer Study Questions Page 2

Chapters 5-6
1. How does Gram describe Mrs. Jackson.
2. How does Maybeth read?
3. What did one of Mina's friends call Dicey?
4. What was Sammy's opinion of the boys who climbed the swingset?
5. About what does Dicey keep nagging James?
6. Why did Maybeth come home from school crying, and what effect did that have on James?
7. What did Dicey think of her report card grade in English?
8. How did Millie describe Gram as a girl?
9. Why didn't Dicey like the bet Sammy made?
10. Why did Miss Eversleigh give Dicey an F on her assignment? Why was that ironic?

Chapters 7-8
1. Before handing back the students' papers, why does Mr. Chappelle go over the mistakes most people made?
2. By whom does Dicey think the other essay is written?
3. What did Dicey think when everyone was quiet after Mr. Chappelle read her essay?
4. Of what did Mr. Chappelle accuse Dicey?
5. Why did Mr. Chappelle change Dicey's grade and apologize to her?
6. How did Gram describe her husband, John?
7. What does Gram regret about her life with her own family?
8. When Jeff asks if her essay was as good as everyone said it was, what is Dicey's reply?
9. Why was Mina surprised that Dicey had a job?
10. Why couldn't Sammy ride the bus?
11. What illegal profession did the Tillermans used to have?
12. What are Dicey's conversations with Mina like?

Chapters 9-10
1. How did Gram surprise Sammy at school?
2. Why does Dicey think that she should maybe pay attention more in home ec class?
3. What did Gram celebrate with pie and ice cream?
4. What did Gram say to Mina's father? What did she mean?
5. Why did Mina's mother say that Gram was a "lady--no question"?
6. Why did Dicey refuse to go to the dance with Jeff?
7. How do Gram and Dicey afford to go to Boston?
8. What did Mr. Lingerle give Gram?
9. Why did Gram rush up to Boston?
10. Why didn't Dicey buy Maybeth a fancy doll at the toy store?
11. To what did Dicey compare the books in the bookstore?
12. What did Dicey buy Sammy?
13. Why wasn't the man at the wood shop sure he wanted to sell the chess set?
14. Why does Dicey feel comfortable talking about Momma to the sales man at the wood shop?

Dicey's Song Short Answer Study Questions Page 3

Chapters 11-12
1. Why didn't Gram get an urn at the undertaker's place?
2. How did Gram react to the wood shop salesman's offering her the wooden box for free?
3. Who did Dicey want to find for Gram?
4. Who came to meet Dicey and Gram at the train station?
5. Where did they bury Momma?
6. How was Sammy like Bullet?

KEY: SHORT ANSWER STUDY GUIDE QUESTIONS - *Dicey's Song*

Chapters 1-2

1. Describe Dicey.
    Dicey is 13 years old. She is hardworking, devoted, unselfish, and she gives much more than she takes.

2. What does Dicey consider her "pot of gold"?
    The sailboat is her pot of gold.

3. How does Dicey feel about school?
    She feels that "about all school was good for was using up your days."

4. What did people say about Maybeth?
    People say she is retarded, though Dicey feels that she is only shy, slow and frightened.

5. What was Gram's transportation to go downtown?
    She drove her boat.

6. Name and give the ages of Dicey's brothers.
    James is ten and Sammy is seven.

7. What does Dicey say Maybeth looks like?
    She says Maybeth looks like a Christmas angel with her wide, hazel eyes and her soft hair and her quiet ways.

8. From whom and how did Dicey get a job?
    Dicey went to see Millie Tydings, the woman who owned the local grocery store. She offered to clean Millie's store each afternoon. She argued that if the store were clean, Millie would have more business, which would more than pay for Dicey's work.

9. Where did Gram and the children live?
    They live in Crisfield, Maryland on the Chesapeake Bay.

10. From whom was Maybeth's note, and what did it say?
    The note was from her music teacher, asking for a conference.

11. Who was Dicey's English teacher?
    Mr. Chappelle was the English teacher.

12. Who did Dicey think was the only interesting girl in her class?
    She thought Wilhemina was interesting.

13. Who did Dicey meet after school?
    She met a boy who played the guitar and sang songs.

14. How did Dicey and Wilhemina get acquainted?
    They worked together on a science project.

Chapters 3-4

1. What important letter came in October?
    A letter came from Boston, from the hospital where Momma was staying.

2. Where was Dicey's old home?
    Dicey and the other children used to live in Provincetown on the Cape with their mother until she became too ill to care for them.

3. What was Gram's response to the letter from Boston?
    She decided to go ahead with the adoption of the children.

4. Why does Dicey feel that she doesn't have to worry about Sammy?
    He appears to be better adjusted since he isn't fighting with kids at school like he used to in Provincetown.

5. Who is Jeff?
    Jeff is the guitar player Dicey sees after school.

6. Why does Millie always make mistakes on the order forms?
    She makes mistakes because she cannot read.

7. What was Maybeth's talent?
    Maybeth had a talent for music -- for playing the piano and singing.

8. About whom does Dicey want to write her English composition?
    She thinks of Will Hawkins and Momma, and decides to write about Momma.

9. How does Dicey feel about cousin Eunice?
    She thinks Eunice is a boring person, and that she only took the children to make people think she did the right thing.

10. What does Dicey first notice about Mr. Lingerle?
    She notices that he is fat -- so fat that his fanny hangs off of the piano bench.

11. Why did Dicey almost protest when Gram asked Mr. Lingerle for dinner?
    She worried that they would never have enough food to feed him.

12. How did Dicey feel when everyone laughed at her home-ec apron?
    She didn't care.

13. What did Mina count on Dicey not to be?
    She counted on Dicey's not being ordinary.

14. How does Gram feel about getting welfare checks?
    She doesn't like to get them because it makes her have to let go of her pride. She would rather be self-sufficient.

15. How did Gram respond to Dicey's question about the conferences?
    She put Dicey off until later.

16. How did James and the other children get into trouble with Gram?
    They got caught looking at her things in the attic without first asking her permission.

17. Why did Gram and Dicey go to Salisbury?
    They went to buy some clothes and things the children needed. They also used the time to talk about the conferences.

18. What is Maybeth's problem in school?
    Although she is working hard, she is not progressing in her studies.

19. How would Momma react to Maybeth's problem?
    Dicey says she would just pretend that Maybeth had no problem.

Chapters 5-6

1. How does Gram describe Mrs. Jackson.
    She says Mrs. Jackson is one of those people who thinks that if you work hard enough everything will go your way.

2. How does Maybeth read?
    She reads the beginning of the word and guesses the rest.

3. What did one of Mina's friends call Dicey?
    She called her "honky."

4. What was Sammy's opinion of the boys who climbed the swingset?
    He thought they climbed the swingset to get in trouble so they would get out of taking the math test that day.

5. About what does Dicey keep nagging James?
    She nags him about finding a way to teach Maybeth to read.

6. Why did Maybeth come home from school crying, and what effect did that have on James?
    She came home crying because the children laughed at her reading. James then realized that Maybeth needed his help immediately, and he went to work on finding a way to teach her to read.

7. What did Dicey think of her report card grade in English?
    She thought it must be a mistake because she had received As and Bs on all of her assignments.

8. How did Millie describe Gram as a girl?
   She said Gram was a girl who would keep things happening.

9. Why didn't Dicey like the bet Sammy made?
   She didn't like it because it wasn't fair to him. She thought the other boys were taking advantage of Sammy.

10. Why did Miss Eversleigh give Dicey an F on her assignment? Why was that ironic?
    Miss Eversleigh thought that no one could live long on Dicey's meals. That was ironic because in fact Dicey and the children <u>did</u> live on those meals.

Chapters 7-8

1. Before handing back the students' papers, why does Mr. Chappelle go over the mistakes most people made?
   He knows no one would listen to him afterwards.

2. By whom does Dicey think the other essay is written?
   She thinks it is written by Mina, and she is right.

3. What did Dicey think when everyone was quiet after Mr. Chappelle read her essay?
   She thought everyone liked it.

4. Of what did Mr. Chappelle accuse Dicey?
   He said she plagiarized her essay, and he gave her a failing grade.

5. Why did Mr. Chappelle change Dicey's grade and apologize to her?
   He did so because Mina made him see that Dicey had not plagiarized her essay.

6. How did Gram describe her husband, John?
   She said John was a stiff, proud, hard man.

7. What does Gram regret about her life with her own family?
   She regrets that she never "reached out" to her own family; she just let them drift away.

8. When Jeff asks if her essay was as good as everyone said it was, what is Dicey's reply?
   She says, "No, of course not, but it was good."

9. Why was Mina surprised that Dicey had a job?
   Besides the fact that Dicey had never mentioned it to her, Mina knew Dicey was too young to get a work permit.

10. Why couldn't Sammy ride the bus?
    He got suspended from riding the bus because he was in a fight.

11. What illegal profession did the Tillermans used to have?
    They used to be bootleggers.

12. What are Dicey's conversations with Mina like?
    They are "like running along the ocean." Mina has a quick mind, and she keeps a constant barrage of varied topics going.

Chapters 9-10

1. How did Gram surprise Sammy at school?
    Gram went to Sammy's school and played marbles with the second graders. She won everyone's marbles -- even Sammy's.

2. Why does Dicey think that she should maybe pay attention more in home ec class?
    She thinks about all the things Gram has been able to do for them and how valuable her skills have been. She decides she would like to know how to do these things just in case she would ever need to do them.

3. What did Gram celebrate with pie and ice cream?
    She celebrated the official adoption of the children.

4. What did Gram say to Mina's father? What did she mean?
    She said, "I've come to put a face on the bogeyman." She meant that she had come to meet them in person so they could make up their own minds about her instead of only hearing rumors about her.

5. Why did Mina's mother say that Gram was a "lady--no question"?
    Gram was one of the few white women who didn't ask Mina's mother if she did cleaning.

6. Why did Dicey refuse to go to the dance with Jeff?
    She knew she was too young to go, and besides, it sounded boring.

7. How do Gram and Dicey afford to go to Boston?
    Gram decides to "sell that wretched cranberry spoon."

8. What did Mr. Lingerle give Gram?
    He gave her an envelope full of money just in case she wouldn't have enough.

9. Why did Gram rush up to Boston?
    Momma was dying, and she wanted to be with her.

10. Why didn't Dicey buy Maybeth a fancy doll at the toy store?
    She didn't buy one because they all had pouty, snooty faces. She thought that if they were real people, you wouldn't like them.

11. To what did Dicey compare the books in the bookstore?
    She compared them to the patients in the hospital. They were all lined up and you didn't know what was inside them.

12. What did Dicey buy Sammy?
    She bought him a toy rocket.

13. Why wasn't the man at the wood shop sure he wanted to sell the chess set?
    This particular chess set had beautiful grain in the wood, and he could not make another set exactly like it.

14. Why does Dicey feel comfortable talking about Momma to the sales man at the wood shop?
    He seemed to genuinely care about her troubles and he sympathized with her.

<u>Chapters 11-12</u>
1. Why didn't Gram get an urn at the undertaker's place?
    She didn't think any of them were right for Momma.

2. How did Gram react to the wood shop salesman's offering her the wooden box for free?
    She was embarrassed, and she had to let go of her pride. She accepted it since it was a gift and was not out of charity.

3. Who did Dicey want to find for Gram?
    She wants to find her Uncle John, Gram's son.

4. Who came to meet Dicey and Gram at the train station?
    Mr. Lingerle brought the kids to meet them.

5. Where did they bury Momma?
    They buried Momma under the paper mulberry tree in Gram's yard.

6. How was Sammy like Bullet?
    Neither child would ever give up on something he wanted.

MULTIPLE CHOICE STUDY GUIDE/QUIZ QUESTIONS - *Dicey's Song*

Chapters 1-2

1. Which of the following does not describe Dicey?
    a. She is 17.
    b. She is hardworking.
    c. She is devoted.
    d. She is unselfish.

2. What does Dicey consider her "pot of gold"?
    a. Her voice.
    b. Her intellect.
    c. Her sailboat.
    d. Her pet horse.

3. How does Dicey feel about school?
    a. She thinks it is very interesting.
    b. She thinks all it does is use up the days.
    c. She hates it.
    d. She enjoys science, but dislikes all the other subjects.

4. What did people say about Maybeth?
    a. She was conceited
    b. She was shy and scared
    c. She was talented.
    d. She was retarded.

5. What was Gram's transportation to go downtown?
    a. She rode on her bicycle.
    b. She walked.
    c. She drove her boat.
    d. She rode a horse.

6. How old are Dicey's brothers?
    a. James is ten and Sammy is seven.
    b. James is fourteen and Sammy is eleven.
    c. James is thirteen and Sammy is eight.
    d. James is twelve and Sammy is seven.

7. What does Dicey say Maybeth looks like?
    a. A Japanese doll
    b. An Eskimo
    c. A movie star
    d. A Christmas angel

Dicey Multiple Choice Study/Quiz Questions Page 2

8. How did Dicey convince Millie Tydings to give her a job?
    a. She told her that if the store were cleaner she would have more business.
    b. She told her what a good worker she would be, and that she would work for less than minimum wage.
    c. She said she would also clean Millie's house for free every week.
    d. She told her that her brothers would also come and help for free.

9. Where did Gram and the children live?
    a. Sausalito, California on the San Francisco Bay
    b. Crisfield, Maryland on the Chesapeake Bay
    c. Sanibel Island, Florida on the Gulf of Mexico
    d. Cape Cod, off the coast of Massachusetts

10. From whom was Maybeth's note, and what did it say?
    a. It was from a boy in class who liked her, asking if he could visit her.
    b. It was from her music teacher, asking for a conference.
    c. It was from her mother, telling her to keep up the good work.
    d. It was from Gram, and was a list of groceries she was to get on the way home from school.

11. What did Mr. Chappelle teach?
    a. Math
    b. Science
    c. Home Economics
    d. English

12. What did Dicey think of Wilhemina?
    a. She was jealous of her good fortune.
    b. She thought Wilhemina was a snob.
    c. She thought Wilhemina was interesting.
    d. She didn't like Wilhemina because she flirted with boys.

13. Who did Dicey meet after school?
    a. Mr. Chappelle
    b. A boy who played the guitar and sang
    c. Wilhemina and her friends
    d. The town librarian

14. How did Dicey and Wilhemina get acquainted?
    a. They worked together on a science project.
    b. They walked home from school together.
    c. They cleaned the classroom together.
    d. They played ball after school.

Dicey Multiple Choice Study/Quiz Questions Page 3

Chapters 3-4

15. True or False: In October a letter came from the hospital in Boston where Dicey's mother was staying.
    a. True
    b. False

16. Where was Dicey's old home?
    a. Provincetown, on Cape Cod
    b. Cambridge, Massachusetts
    c. Downtown Boston
    d. Marblehead, a small fishing town near Boston

17. What was Gram's response to the letter?
    a. She decided to send the children back to their mother.
    b. She decided to go ahead with the adoption of the children.
    c. She cried and became depressed.
    d. She immediately called the children's mother on the phone.

18. How does Dicey feel about Sammy?
    a. She feels she doesn't have to worry about him; he is adjusting well to school.
    b. She is worried because he is fighting with the other children and is not adjusting to his new situation.
    c. She is afraid he will take the sailboat out on the bay by himself and have an accident.
    d. She is angry with him because he will not do anything she tells him.

19. Who is Jeff?
    a. He is the captain of the football team, who seems to like Dicey.
    b. He is the bag boy who works at Millie's store.
    c. He is Gram's next door neighbor.
    d. He is the guitar player Dicey sees after school.

20. Why does Millie always make mistakes on the order forms?
    a. She needs glasses but refuses to get them.
    b. She has a drinking problem which affects her vision.
    c. She cannot read.
    d. She is always trying to do more than one thing at a time and doesn't pay attention to what she is doing.

21. What is Maybeth's talent?
    a. She is a ventriloquist.
    b. She plays the piano and sings.
    c. She is a talented gymnast.
    d. She is a mathematics whiz.

Dicey Multiple Choice Study/Quiz Questions Page 4

22. About whom does Dicey write her English composition.
    a. Momma
    b. Jeff
    c. Sammy and Maybeth
    d. Will Hawkins

23. How does Dicey feel about cousin Eunice?
    a. She thinks Eunice is interesting, as well as kind and loving.
    b. She thinks Eunice is boring, and that she only took the children to make people think she did the right thing.
    c. She resents Eunice's insinuations about her mother.
    d. She doesn't trust Eunice; she thinks Eunice is an evil person.

24. What does Dicey first notice about Mr. Lingerle?
    a. He wears a wig.
    b. He bites his nails.
    c. He smells like garlic.
    d. He is so fat his fanny hangs over the piano bench.

25. Why did Dicey almost protest when Gram asked Mr. Lingerle to stay for dinner?
    a. She had a lot of homework and did not want to have to entertain a guest.
    b. She thought Gram was working too hard and should not go to the extra trouble of preparing a big dinner.
    c. She was afraid they would not have enough food to feed him.
    d. She worried that he would criticize Gram's cooking, and insult her.

26. How does Dicey feel when everyone laughs at her apron?
    a. She takes it personally and is quite hurt.
    b. She doesn't care.
    c. She breaks down into tears right in front of the class.
    d. She vows to wreck as many of the other kids' projects as possible for the rest of the year.

27. What does Mina count on Dicey not to be?
    a. Late
    b. Conceited
    c. Ordinary
    d. Boy-crazy

28. How does Gram feel about getting welfare checks?
    a. She is glad to have the extra income to help her take care of the children.
    b. She doesn't like it because she would rather be self-sufficient.
    c. She figures that she has worked all of her life when she could, and that she deserves every penny she is getting.
    d. She doesn't like politicians or the government, but she gladly takes their money.

Dicey Multiple Choice Study/Quiz Questions Page 5

29. How does Gram respond to Dicey's question about the conference?
    a. She puts Dicey off until later.
    b. She responds immediately.
    c. She reprimands Dicey and tells her she cannot stay after school for two weeks.
    d. She smiles and gives her another helping of pie.

30. How do James and the other children get in trouble with Gram?
    a. They take food from the refrigerator.
    b. They take money from Gram's purse.
    c. They look at her things in the attic without asking permission first.
    d. They go fishing after school without telling her where they are going.

31. Why did Gram and Dicey go to Salisbury?
    a. To open a bank account for Dicey
    b. To send a telegram to Momma
    c. To look for a job for Gram
    d. To buy clothes and things for the children

32. What is Maybeth's problem in school?
    a. She refuses to do any work.
    b. She is so far ahead that she is bored and is becoming a behavior problem.
    c. She works hard but does not make any progress.
    d. She cries all of the time and can't seem to concentrate on her work.

33. How would Momma react to Maybeth's problem?
    a. She would beat Maybeth and tell her to straighten up.
    b. She would pretend there was no problem.
    c. She would help Maybeth solve the problem.
    d. She would ask for help from the teacher.

Dicey Multiple Choice Study/Quiz Questions Page 6

<u>Chapters 5-6</u>

34. Gram thinks Mr. Jackson is one of those people who thinks that . . .
    a. . . . if you work hard enough everything will go your way.
    b. . . . no matter how hard you work you will never get ahead without luck.
    c. . . . it doesn't matter whether you work or not; your fate is predetermined.
    d. . . . if you dress nicely and are polite, you don't need any other education.

35. How does Maybeth read?
    a. She memorizes a few words and says them over and over.
    b. She looks at the pictures and makes up a story.
    c. She reads the beginning of the word and guesses at the rest.
    d. She asks the children around her to help her.

36. What does one of Mina's friends call Dicey?
    a. Dirty Yankee
    b. Honky
    c. White Trash
    d. Dopey Dicey

37. True or False: Sammy thought the boys climbed the swing set to impress the girls and show how brave they were.
    a. True
    b. False

38. About what does Dicey keep nagging James?
    a. Helping her find a boyfriend
    b. Brushing his teeth and keeping himself clean
    c. Doing his household chores
    d. Teaching Maybeth to read

39. True or False: Maybeth came home crying because the other children laughed at her singing.
    a. True
    b. False

40. What does Dicey think of her report card grade in English?
    a. She thinks it must be a mistake.
    b. She thinks it is a fair grade.
    c. She thinks her teacher is just trying to make her work harder.
    d. She doesn't care about the grade at all; she thinks school is useless, anyway, and doesn't care whether she gets good grades or not.

Dicey Multiple Choice Study/Quiz Questions Page 7

41. How does Millie describe Gram as a girl?
    a. Gram was shy and quiet.
    b. Gram would keep things happening.
    c. Gram was intense and studious.
    d. Gram was a loner who had no friends.

42. How does Dicey feel about the bet Sammy made?
    a. She thinks he will win easily and that he is taking advantage of the other boys.
    b. She thinks it is unfair to him, and the other boys are taking advantage of him.
    c. She doesn't like gambling of any kind, regardless of who wins or loses or whether or not the bet is fair.
    d. She is sad that Sammy has chosen a morally corrupt path at such a young age.

43. Why was Dicey's grade of F on the assignment from Miss Eversleigh ironic?
    a. It was the only F Dicey had ever received.
    b. Gram had done the assignment for Dicey.
    c. Miss Eversleigh thought that no one could survive on those meals, but Dicey and the children did.
    d. Dicey had followed Miss Eversleigh's directions and advice exactly, yet Miss Eversleigh did not recognize it. She had actually given a failing grade to her own ideas.

Dicey Multiple Choice Study/Quiz Questions Page 8

Chapters 7-8

44. Before handing back the students' papers, why does Mr. Chappelle go over the mistakes most people made?
    a. He thinks most of the students will erase the wrong answers and put in the correct ones if they have their papers when he is going over the answers. He is afraid they will try to tell him they had the correct answers when they did not.
    b. He knows no one will listen to him after he gives back the papers.
    c. He does not want to have to teach anything else that day, so he wastes time by going over the answers.
    d. It is a rule made by the principal, and all of the teachers have to follow it.

45. By whom does Dicey think the other essay is written?
    a. Jeff
    b. Wilhemina
    c. Mina
    d. Mr. Chappelle -- as a trick

46. What does Dicey think when everyone is quiet after Mr. Chappelle reads her essay?
    a. Everyone hates it.
    b. No one paid attention.
    c. Everyone likes it.
    d. They are being rude to her on purpose.

47. Of what does Mr. Chappelle accuse Dicey?
    a. Plagiarism
    b. Slander
    c. Conspiracy
    d. Bribery

48. How is the situation between Dicey and Mr. Chappelle resolved?
    a. Dicey accepts the grade even though she disagrees with him.
    b. Mina makes him see that his judgement is incorrect, and he changes the grade.
    c. Dicey and Gram go to the principal and make a formal complaint to get the grade changed.
    d. Dicey does the work over and gets a new grade.

49. How does Gram describe her husband, John?
    a. A kind, loving man
    b. Lazy and shiftless
    c. A good worker but not very bright
    d. A stiff, hard, proud man

Dicey Multiple Choice Study/Quiz Questions Page 9

50. What does Gram regret?
    a. That she never reached out to her own family; she let them just drift away.
    b. That she married John.
    c. That she adopted the children.
    d. That she stopped getting welfare checks.

51. When Jeff asks if her essay was as good as everyone else's, what is Dicey's reply?
    a. "Yes, it was every bit as good as the best of them."
    b. "No, of course not, but it was good."
    c. "I don't know; why don't you read it and see for yourself."
    d. "I don't know, but writing it made me feel better, so I guess it doesn't matter how it stacks up against the others in the class."

52. Why was Mina surprised that Dicey had a job?
    a. Dicey never wore nice clothes, so it did not look like she had any money to spend.
    b. Dicey didn't seem to have enough energy to hold down a job.
    c. Dicey wasn't old enough to have a work permit.
    d. Dicey had not lived in the area very long, and usually the jobs were only given to the "locals."

53. Why couldn't Sammy ride the bus?
    a. He got sick in moving vehicles.
    b. He didn't have enough money to pay for it.
    c. He lived close enough to school to walk.
    d. He got suspended because he was in a fight.

54. What illegal profession did the Tillermans used to have?
    a. Slave traders
    b. Counterfeiters
    c. Bootleggers
    d. Robbers

55. What are Dicey's conversations with Mina like?
    a. "Pulling teeth"
    b. "Running along the ocean"
    c. "A rainbow after a storm"
    d. "Trying to walk through quicksand"

Dicey Multiple Choice Study/Quiz Questions Page 10

<u>Chapters 9-10</u>

56. What did Gram do at school?
    a. Played marbles
    b. Talked about some of the history of the town and its people
    c. Played ball
    d. Had a conference with Sammy's bus driver

57. True or False: Dicey thinks the things they are learning in Home Economics are a waste of time. She doesn't think she will ever use them.
    a. True
    b. False

58. How did Gram celebrate the official adoption of the children?
    a. She took them out to dinner.
    b. She put a big sign on the front porch for all of her neighbors to see.
    c. She gave them all pie and ice cream.
    d. She took them to church and offered prayers of thanksgiving.

59. True or False: Gram said that if Mina's father was curious about her, he should come to visit her.
    a. True
    b. False

60. Why did Mina's mother say Gram was "a lady--no question"?
    a. Gram always addressed people as "Mr." or "Mrs."
    b. Gram always got dressed up and wore white gloves when she went calling.
    c. Gram never used profanity.
    d. Gram was one of the few white women who never asked Mina's mother if she did cleaning.

61. Why does Dicey refuse to go to the dance with Jeff?
    a. She doesn't have enough money to buy a dress, but she doesn't want to admit it.
    b. She is embarrassed to tell Gram she likes Jeff.
    c. She knows she is too young, and it sounds boring.
    d. She wouldn't go unless Mina had a date, too.

62. How do Gram and Dicey afford to go to Boston?
    a. They take in cleaning and sewing to make the extra money.
    b. They ask the pastor of their church to help them out.
    c. They skimp on food to save money.
    d. Gram sells a spoon.

Dicey Multiple Choice Study/Quiz Questions Page 11

63. What does Mr. Lingerle give Gram?
    a. His credit card
    b. An envelope full of money
    c. The name of a friend in Boston who will let them stay with her for free
    d. A diamond ring she can sell if she needs to

64. True or False: Gram rushes to Boston to bring Momma back home with her.
    a. True
    b. False

65. True or False: Dicey bought Maybeth a beautiful doll at the toy store.
    a. True
    b. False

66. To what did Dicey compare the books in the bookstore?
    a. Soldiers on the battlefield
    b. Flowers getting ready to bloom
    c. Patients in the hospital
    d. Trees in the forest

67. What did Dicey buy Sammy?
    a. A puppy
    b. A fishing rod
    c. A jackknife
    d. A toy rocket

68. Why wasn't the man at the wood shop sure he wanted to sell the chess set?
    a. The chess set had a beautiful grain in the wood, and he could not make another one exactly like it.
    b. He thought he might be able to get more money for it from someone who looked richer than Dicey.
    c. He was thinking of giving it to his grandson for a present.
    d. It had belonged to his father, and he had a great sentimental attachment to it.

69. Does Dicey feel comfortable talking to the salesman at the wood shop?
    a. Yes, it is easy to talk to him because he is a stranger.
    b. Yes, he reminds her of her father.
    c. No, he is a rather stiff and stern man.
    d. No, she is a little scared of him.

Dicey Multiple Choice Study/Quiz Questions Page 12

Chapters 11-12

70. Why doesn't Gram get an urn at the undertaker's place?
    a. She can't afford it.
    b. The undertaker is sold out of the kind she wants.
    c. She doesn't think any of them are right for Momma.
    d. She is too upset to admit that Momma is dead.

71. How does Gram react to the wood shop salesman's offer to give her the wooden box for free?
    a. She lets go of her pride and accepts it as a gift, not charity.
    b. She becomes proud and stubborn and refuses it.
    c. She breaks down into tears at such a beautiful, thoughtful gesture.
    d. She recognizes that it is charity and accepts it, but she feels disappointed in herself and becomes depressed.

72. What does Dicey want to do for Gram?
    a. She wants to buy Gram a new dress.
    b. She wants to take Gram to the beauty parlor to have her hair done.
    c. She wants to find Gram's son.
    d. She wants to take the place of the daughter Gram lost.

73. Who comes to meet Dicey and Gram at the train station?
    a. Jeff
    b. Mina and her parents
    c. No one
    d. Mr. Lingerle and the kids

74. Where do they bury Momma?
    a. They spread her ashes out over the water.
    b. They bury her under the mulberry tree in Gram's yard.
    c. They bury her in the town cemetery.
    d. They bury her next to a rose bush she planted when she was a child.

75. True or False: Sammy and Bullet are alike because neither would ever give up on something he wanted.
    a. True
    b. False

ANSWER KEY - MULTIPLE CHOICE STUDY/QUIZ QUESTIONS
Dicey's Song

Chapters 1-2	Chapters 3-4	Chapters 5-6	Chapters 7-8
1. A	15. A	34. A	44. B
2. C	16. A	35. C	45. C
3. B	17. B	36. B	46. C
4. D	18. A	37. B	47. A
5. C	19. D	38. D	48. B
6. A	20. C	39. B	49. D
7. D	21. B	40. A	50. A
8. A	22. A	41. B	51. B
9. B	23. B	42. B	52. C
10. B	24. D	43. C	53. D
11. D	25. C		54. C
12. C	26. B		55. B
13. B	27. C		
14. A	28. B		
	29. A		
	30. C		
	31. D		
	32. C		
	33. B		

Chapters 9-10	Chapters 11-12
56. A	70. C
57. B	71. A
58. C	72. C
59. B	73. D
60. D	74. B
61. C	75. A
62. D	
63. B	
64. B	
65. B	
66. C	
67. D	
68. A	
69. A	

PREREADING VOCABULARY WORKSHEETS

VOCABULARY - *Dicey's Song*

<u>Chapters 1 & 2</u> Part I: Using Prior Knowledge and Contextual Clues

Below are sentences in which the vocabulary words appear in the text. Read the sentence. Use any clues you can find in the sentence combined with your prior knowledge, and write what you think the underlined words mean on the lines provided.

1. "We'll do fractions after dinner," she promised Maybeth, who nodded with no more <u>enthusiasm</u> than Dicey felt.

   _____

2. It would be more <u>convenient</u> for people to come to you.

   _____

3. Dicey hurried through them, but Maybeth <u>lingered</u>, humming.

   _____

4. She liked the <u>precision</u> of it.

   _____

5. "John Wilkes Booth," Wilhemina announced <u>triumphantly.</u>

   _____

6. "Between someone and himself," she said, not bothering to keep the anger at his <u>intrusion</u> out of her voice.

   _____

7. He looked <u>chastened</u> and sulky.

   _____

8. He looked chastened and <u>sulky</u>.

   _____

Part II Determining the Meaning   Match the vocabulary words to their dictionary definitions.

   ___ 1. enthusiasm   A. easy to do, use, or get to; easily accessible
   ___ 2. convenient   B. showing resentment and ill humor; sullen
   ___ 3. lingered   C. exactness
   ___ 4. precision   D. intense or eager interest; passion
   ___ 5. triumphantly   E. subdued; restrained from excess
   ___ 6. intrusion   F. an invasion of privacy
   ___ 7. chastened   G. continue to stay; delayed; loitered
   ___ 8. sulky   H. successfully; elated

Vocabulary - *Dicey's Song* Chapters 3 & 4

Part I: Using Prior Knowledge and Contextual Clues

Below are sentences in which the vocabulary words appear in the text. Read the sentence. Use any clues you can find in the sentence combined with your prior knowledge, and write what you think the underlined words mean on the lines provided.

1. She stopped and listened, <u>dumbfounded</u>.

   _____

2. Mr. Lingerle gave Dicey a curious look, then he gave Gram a curious look, and his eyes became less <u>wary</u>.

   _____

3. <u>Vaguely</u>, she wondered what they could be quarreling about.

   _____

4. I'd forgotten that when you leave children alone they have a natural <u>tendency</u> to get into trouble.

   _____

5. Then the grayness, the papers blowing on sidewalks, the sandy-colored sameness of the buildings <u>diminished</u> that excitement.

   _____

6. Others were <u>meandering</u> about, stopping at store windows, as if they had a whole day to kill.

   _____

7. "We'll <u>confer</u> with James when we get home, but I wanted---besides, we never get to talk much, do we."

   _____

8. They were in the same poses as the <u>mannikins</u> for ladies, which Dicey thought was pretty stupid.

   _____

Part II: Determining the Meaning   Match the vocabulary words to their dictionary definitions.

___ 1. dumbfounded   A. an aimless wandering; rambling
___ 2. wary   B. inclination to move or act in a particular way
___ 3. vaguely   C. not sharp or certain; hazily
___ 4. tendency   D. models of the human body used in stores
___ 5. diminished   E. to have a conference or talk
___ 6. meandering   F. cautious; on one's guard
___ 7. confer   G. made smaller; lessened; reduced
___ 8. mannikins   H. to make speechless by shocking; amazed

Vocabulary - *Dicey's Song* Chapters 5 & 6

Part I: Using Prior Knowledge and Contextual Clues
    Below are the sentences in which the vocabulary words appear in the text.
Read the sentence. Use any clues you can find in the sentence combined with your prior knowledge, and write what you think the underlined words mean on the lines provided.

1. He hesitated, rocking up and back to get out of the chair, then sitting back, then lurching forward
_____

2. Miss Eversleigh stood in front of the class wearing her usual dark suit and usual nylon blouse with her usual pin on the lapel of her jacket.
_____

3. My theory is, all that stuff interfered with her before and it won't interfere now.
_____

4. Dicey listened hard, not to hear precisely what they were saying, but to hear what the two speakers were like.
_____

5. It was something called a minuet, by someone called Bach.
_____

6. He carried his guitar slung over his back, like a minstrel out of Robin Hood.
_____

7. They said in my book that learning to read with phrasing and fluently, that was a sure sign.
_____

8. She concentrated on that, anticipating what he would say about hers, feeling proud and glad.
_____

Part II: Determining the Meaning   Match the vocabulary words to their dictionary definitions.

____ 1. lurching   A. looking forward to or expecting
____ 2. lapel   B. a travelling poet, singer or musician
____ 3. interfere   C. write or speak easily, smoothly and expressively
____ 4. precisely   D. rolling, pitching or swaying suddenly; staggering
____ 5. minuet   E. part of a jacket folded back from the neckline
____ 6. minstrel   F. meddle; hinder, prevent; intervene
____ 7. fluently   G. particularly; mainly; to a marked degree
____ 8. anticipating   H. a slow, stately dance or the music for the dance

Vocabulary - *Dicey's Song* Chapters 7 & 8

Part I: Using Prior Knowledge and Contextual Clues

Below are the sentences in which the vocabulary words appear in the text.
Read the sentence. Use any clues you can find in the sentence combined with your prior knowledge, and write what you think the underlined words mean on the lines provided.

1. The ocean rolled up toward her rickety cabin, like it wanted to swallow it up; but it never did.

   _____

2. In the first place, her tongue felt like it was frozen solid, and her head was a block of ice, and all the blood in her body had chilled and congealed.

   _____

3. "What I primarily resent is the deceitfulness of it, the cheap trickery, the lies," Mr. Chappelle declared.

   _____

4. But behind the liquid darkness of Mina's eyes, Dicey saw mischief.

   _____

5. Jeff answered briefly that his father insisted that kids sit in the back, where it was safer for them.

   _____

6. Mr. Lingerle lifted his face and halted his laden fork at mid-journey to his mouth.

   _____

7. Each of the many ounces of flesh that made up his body seemed to emanate comfort, contentment, good will.

   _____

8. The cold weather had been nudged aside by an unexpectedly balmy day.

   _____

Part II: Determining the Meaning   Match the vocabulary words to their dictionary definitions.

___ 1. rickety   A. to declare firmly and persistently
___ 2. congealed   B. teasing; prank; naughty; a troublesome act
___ 3. deceitfulness   C. loaded; burdened
___ 4. mischief   D. to flow out; come forth; emit
___ 5. insisted   E. coagulated; solidified or thickened by cooling
___ 6. laden   F. soothing; mild; pleasant
___ 7. emanate   G. liable to fall or break down because of weakness
___ 8. balmy   H. dishonest action or trick; fraud or lie

Vocabulary - *Dicey's Song* Chapters 9, 10, 11 and 12

Part I: Using Prior Knowledge and Contextual Clues
  Below are the sentences in which the vocabulary words appear in the text.
Read the sentence. Use any clues you can find in the sentence combined with your prior knowledge, and write what you think the underlined words mean on the lines provided.

1. "Yeah, but I've got charisma," Mina argued.

_____

2. If it was good news, and Gram was trying not to be optimistic so she wouldn't be disappointed,

_____

3. The place smelled of cleansing liquid and the empty hall reverberated with muffled sounds.

_____

4. Her head lay back on the pillow, surrounded by an aureole of honey-colored hair.

_____

5. The girl behind the counter gave her only one, harried, glance before she filled out the receipt and put the plane and catapult into a box.

_____

6. "If you were to have her cremated and carried her with you," Preston said to Gram

_____

7. "Those bright red hearts, perfectly symmetrical."

_____

8. James didn't look around to contradict this.

_____

Part II: Determining the Meaning   Match the vocabulary words to their dictionary definitions.

___ 1. charisma   A. to be reflected as light or sound waves
___ 2. optimistic   B. exact correspondence of form on opposite sides of a
                                dividing line
___ 3. reverberated   C. tormented or worried; harassed
___ 4. aureole   D. a special quality that inspires allegiance and devotion
___ 5. harried   E. expect the best outcome
___ 6. cremated   F. burnt up; to burn a dead body to ashes
___ 7. symmetrical   G. a radiance encircling the head or body; a halo
___ 8. contradict   H. oppose verbally; go against; assert the opposite

ANSWER KEY - VOCABULARY
Dicey's Song

Chapters 1 & 2	Chapters 3 & 4	Chapters 5 & 6	Chapters 7 & 8	Chapters 9-12
1. D	1. H	1. D	1. G	1. D
2. A	2. F	2. E	2. E	2. E
3. G	3. C	3. F	3. H	3. A
4. C	4. B	4. G	4. B	4. G
5. H	5. G	5. H	5. A	5. C
6. F	6. A	6. B	6. C	6. F
7. E	7. E	7. C	7. D	7. B
8. B	8. D	8. A	8. F	8. H

DAILY LESSONS

LESSON ONE

Objectives
1. To introduce the *Dicey's Song* unit.
2. To distribute books and other related materials
3. To preview the study questions for chapters 1-2
4. To familiarize students with the vocabulary for chapters 1-2

Activity #1

Ask students for a show of hands of those who have at some time in the past moved and changed schools or neighborhoods. Ask these students from where they moved and what things were like at their old neighborhoods. (This works especially well if a few students have moved in from different states, or places substantially different from your community.)

As a transition, note that the novel students are about to read is about a girl, Dicey, and her brothers and sister who move to live with their grandmother.

Activity #2

Explain to students that there is a project assignment that goes along with this unit. The characters in the story are "doers." They all enjoy doing something which has a tangible product. The project assignment is to create something. Some suggestions are: to sew a garment or craft item, to knit or crochet something, to refinish a piece of furniture, to learn a new song to sing or play on an instrument (If several students wish to work together to form a "band" or quartet, that would help self-conscious students to perform), to paint a picture, to build a birdhouse, to make a model, or to compose a poem or a song. Of course, students are not limited to these suggestions; if they have other things they would like to do, they could be acceptable.

Tell students that whatever they create, they will be expected to show it (or perform it) during Lesson Twelve (give them a day and date). Explain the criteria on which their projects will be graded.

Activity #3

Distribute the materials students will use in this unit. Explain in detail how students are to use these materials.

Study Guides Students should read the study guide questions for each reading assignment prior to beginning the reading assignment to get a feeling for what events and ideas are important in the section they are about to read. After reading the section, students will (as a class or individually) answer the questions to review the important events and ideas from that section of the book. Students should keep the study guides as study materials for the unit test.

Vocabulary   Prior to reading a reading assignment, students will do vocabulary work related to the section of the book they are about to read. Following the completion of the reading of the book, there will be a vocabulary review of all the words used in the vocabulary assignments. Students should keep their vocabulary work as study materials for the unit test.

Reading Assignment Sheet   You need to fill in the reading assignment sheet to let students know by when their reading has to be completed. You can either write the assignment sheet up on a side blackboard or bulletin board and leave it there for students to see each day, or you can "ditto" copies for each student to have. In either case, you should advise students to become very familiar with the reading assignments so they know what is expected of them.

Extra Activities Center   The Unit Resource portion of this unit contains suggestions for an extra library of related books and articles in your classroom as well as crossword and word search puzzles. Make an extra activities center in your room where you will keep these materials for students to use. (Bring the books and articles in from the library and keep several copies of the puzzles on hand.) Explain to students that these materials are available for students to use when they finish reading assignments or other class work early.

Nonfiction Assignment Sheet   Explain to students that they each are to read at least one non-fiction piece from the in-class library at some time during the unit. Students will fill out a nonfiction assignment sheet after completing the reading to help you evaluate their reading experiences and to help the students think about and evaluate their own reading experiences.

Books   Each school has its own rules and regulations regarding student use of school books. Advise students of the procedures that are normal for your school.

Activity #4
Show students how to preview the study questions and do the vocabulary work for Chapters 1-2 of *Dicey's Song*. If students do not finish this assignment during this class period, they should complete it prior to the next class meeting.

NONFICTION ASSIGNMENT SHEET - *Dicey's Song*
(To be completed after reading the required nonfiction article)

Name _____ Date _____

Title of Nonfiction Read _____

Written By _____ Publication Date _____

I. Factual Summary: Write a short summary of the piece you read.

II. Vocabulary
    1. With which vocabulary words in the piece did you encounter some degree of difficulty?

    2. How did you resolve your lack of understanding with these words?

III. Interpretation: What was the main point the author wanted you to get from reading his work?

IV. Criticism
    1. With which points of the piece did you agree or find easy to accept? Why?

    2. With which points of the piece did you disagree or find difficult to believe? Why?

V. Personal Response: What do you think about this piece? OR How does this piece influence your ideas?

LESSON TWO

Objectives
1. To read chapters 1-2
2. To give students practice reading orally
3. To evaluate students' oral reading

Activity

Have students read chapters 1-2 of *Dicey's Song* out loud in class. You probably know the best way to get readers with your class; pick students at random, ask for volunteers, or use whatever method works best for your group. If you have not yet completed an oral reading evaluation for your students this marking period, this would be a good opportunity to do so. A form is included with this unit for your convenience. If students do not complete reading chapters 1-2 in class, they should do so prior to your next class meeting.

LESSON THREE

Objectives
1. To review the main events and ideas from chapters 1-2
2. To preview the study questions for chapters 3-4
3. To familiarize students with the vocabulary in chapters 3-4
4. To read chapters 3-4

Activity #1

Give students a few minutes to formulate answers for the study guide questions for chapters 1-2, and then discuss the answers to the questions in detail. Write the answers on the board or overhead transparency so students can have the correct answers for study purposes.

Note: It is a good practice in public speaking and leadership skills for individual students to take charge of leading the discussions of the study questions. Perhaps a different student could go to the front of the class and lead the discussion each day that the study questions are discussed during this unit. Of course, the teacher should guide the discussion when appropriate and be sure to fill in any gaps the students leave.

Activity #2

Give students about fifteen minutes to preview the study questions for chapters 3-4 of *Dicey's Song* and to do the related vocabulary work.

Activity #3

Assign students to read chapters 3-4 of *Dicey's Song* prior to your next class period. If there is time remaining in this period, students may begin reading silently.

ORAL READING EVALUATION - *Dicey's Song*

Name _____ Class _____ Date _____

SKILL	EXCELLENT	GOOD	AVERAGE	FAIR	POOR
Fluency	5	4	3	2	1
Clarity	5	4	3	2	1
Audibility	5	4	3	2	1
Pronunciation	5	4	3	2	1
_____	5	4	3	2	1
_____	5	4	3	2	1

Total _____   Grade _____

Comments:

LESSON FOUR

Objectives
1. To check to see that students read chapters 3-4 as assigned
2. To review the main ideas and events from chapters 3-4
3. To preview the study questions for chapters 5-6
4. To familiarize students with the vocabulary in chapters 5-6
5. To read chapters 5-6
6. To evaluate students' oral reading

Activity #1
   Quiz - Distribute quizzes (multiple choice study questions for chapters 3-4)and give students about 10 minutes to complete them. Have students exchange papers. Grade the quizzes as a class. Collect the papers for recording the grades.

Activity #2
   Give students about 15 minutes to preview the study questions for chapters 5-6 and to do the related vocabulary work.

Activity #3
   Have students read chapters 5-6 orally for the remainder of the class period. Continue the oral reading evaluations. If students do not complete reading these chapters during this class period, they should do so prior to your next class meeting.

LESSON FIVE

Objectives
1. To give students the opportunity to practice writing their own opinions and observations
2. To give the teacher an opportunity to evaluate each student's writing skills

Activity #1
   Distribute Writing Assignment #1 and discuss the directions in detail. Allow the remaining class time for students to complete the assignment. Collect the papers at the end of the class period.

   Follow - Up: After you have graded the assignments, have a writing conference with the students. (This unit schedules one in Lesson Eight.) After the writing conference, allow students to revise their papers using your suggestions and corrections. Give them about three days from the date they receive their papers to complete the revision. I suggest grading the revisions on an A-C-E scale (all revisions well-done, some revisions made, few or no revisions made). This will speed your grading time and still give some credit for the students' efforts.

WRITING ASSIGNMENT #1 - *Dicey's Song*

PROMPT
"He wanted them to write a character sketch, he said, about a real character they had met, someone they knew. He wanted them to show the conflict in a real person's life."

Your assignment is the same as Dicey's (above).

PREWRITING
Dicey gave a lot of thought to her assignment before she began writing. First she brainstormed a bunch of ideas about whom she could write and what she might say about each person. That's a very good first step.

After you decide which person will be the subject of your composition, brainstorm a list of specific things you want to say about that person. Like Dicey, you may choose to change the name of your person so his or her true identity will not be known.

Organize the things you want to say into a logical order, trying to make one idea flow into (or from) another. Make a little outline to follow.

DRAFTING
First, write a paragraph in which you introduce your subject, your character.

In the body of your composition, write several paragraphs about your character, following the outline you made during the prewriting activity above.

Finally, write a concluding paragraph in which you bring together the ideas in your composition and give your final thoughts about your subject.

PROMPT
When you finish the rough draft of your paper, ask a student who sits near you to read it. After reading your rough draft, he/she should tell you what he/she liked best about your work, which parts were difficult to understand, and ways in which your work could be improved. Reread your paper considering your critic's comments, and make the corrections you think are necessary.

PROOFREADING
Do a final proofreading of your paper double-checking your grammar, spelling, organization, and the clarity of your ideas.

LESSON SIX

Objectives
    1. To review the main ideas of chapters 5-6
    2. To preview the study questions and vocabulary for chapters 7-8
    3. To read chapters 7-8

Activity #1

    Ask students to get out their books and some paper (not their study guides). Tell students to write down ten questions (and answers) which cover the main events and ideas in chapters 5-6. Discuss the students questions and answers orally, making a list of the questions with brief responses on the board. Put a star next to the students' questions and answers that are essentially the same as the study guide questions. (Be sure that all the study guide questions are answered.)

Activity #2

    Tell students to do the prereading and reading work for chapters 7-8 prior to your next class meeting. Students may use the remainder of this class period to begin working on this assignment.

LESSON SEVEN

Objectives
    1. To review the main events of chapters 7-8
    2. To check to see that students did the reading assignment
    3. To assign the pre-reading, vocabulary and reading work for chapters 9-10
    4. To give students the opportunity to gather reading materials for the nonfiction reading assignment

Activity #1

    Give students a quiz on chapters 7-8. Use either the short answer or multiple choice form of the study guide questions as a quiz so that in discussing the answers to the quiz you also answer the study guide questions. Collect the papers for grade recording.

Activity #2

    Tell students that prior to Lesson Nine they must have completed the pre-reading, vocabulary and reading work for chapters 9-10. Students may have the remainder of this period to work on this assignment.

Activity #3

    Take students to the library. Tell them that this is their opportunity to gather nonfiction reading materials for their nonfiction reading assignment as well as materials they may need to help them work on their projects.

LESSON EIGHT

Objectives

    1. To evaluate students' writing
    2. To have students revise their first writing assignment papers
    3. To give students the opportunity to practice writing to inform
    4. To help students prepare for their project presentations

Activity #1

    Distribute Writing Assignment #2. Discuss the directions in detail and give students ample time to complete the assignment. It might be a good idea to wait unit after students make their project presentations to collect this writing assignment. If students are (for whatever good reasons) not able to work on this assignment yet, they should continue working on the nonfiction reading assignment or work on reading chapters 9-10 in *Dicey's Song*.

Activity #2

    Call students to your desk (or some other private area) to discuss their papers from Writing Assignment 1. A Writing Evaluation Form is included with this until to help structure your conferences.

LESSON NINE

Objectives

    1. To review the main ideas and events of chapters 9-10
    2. To preview the study questions for chapters 11-12
    3. To do the vocabulary work for chapters 11-12
    4. To read chapters 11-12
    5. To complete the oral reading evaluations

Activity #1

    Discuss the answers to the study guide questions for chapters 11-12. Write the answers on the board for students to copy down for study use later.

Activity #2

    Give students about fifteen minutes to preview the study questions for chapters 11-12 and to complete the vocabulary work for those chapters.

Activity #3

    Have students read chapters 11-12 orally in class. If you have not yet completed the oral reading evaluations, this is the time to do so.

WRITING ASSIGNMENT #2 - *Dicey's Song*

PROMPT

You are working on a project -- actually working on *something* about which you will make an oral presentation. You should have your project well underway by now, and it is time to start thinking about your actual presentation. The purpose of this assignment is to help you prepare your presentation. Your assignment is to write a composition in which you state exactly what you are going to do and say in your presentation.

You are all doing such different things, it is hard to give you specific instructions as to how to prepare. However, there are a few general guidelines you can follow and adapt to your own situations:

Your presentation should be in four parts. In Part One, introduce us, your audience, to your project. Tell what you decided to do and why you decided to do it. Part Two will be a demonstration of your project. In Part Three, tell us how you did the project. Part Four should be time allowed for questions and answers about your project.

PREWRITING

Write down a description of what your project is.

Write down several reasons why you decided to do it.

Make a few notes about how you will actually demonstrate your project.

Jot down a few notes about how you did your project. What materials did you need, what steps did you take, and what problems, if any, did you encounter while doing your project?

DRAFTING

In your first paragraph, introduce your project; tell what your project is and why you chose this particular project.

In your second paragraph, tell exactly how you will demonstrate your project.

In paragraph three, explain how you did your project. Tell what kinds of things were involved in the actual *doing* of the project.

In your final paragraph make your concluding remarks and invite questions from your audience.

PROMPT

When you finish the rough draft of your paper, ask a student who sits near you to read it. After reading your rough draft, he/she should tell you what he/she liked best about your work, which parts were difficult to understand, and ways in which your work could be improved. Reread your paper considering your critic's comments, and make the corrections you think are necessary.

PROOFREADING

Do a final proofreading of your paper double-checking your grammar, spelling, organization, and the clarity of your ideas.

WRITING EVALUATION FORM - *Dicey's Song*

Name _____ Date _____

    Grade _____

Circle One For Each Item:

Grammar:	excellent	good	fair	poor
Spelling:	excellent	good	fair	poor
Punctuation:	excellent	good	fair	poor
Legibility:	excellent	good	fair	poor

Strengths:

Weaknesses:

Comments/Suggestions:

LESSON TEN

Objectives
    1. To check students' understanding of the novel
    2. To give students the opportunity to do some creative writing

Activity

    Explain to students that their assignment is to write "Dicey's Song." They should find an appropriate tune and rewrite the lyrics to match something that would represent "Dicey's Song." If they are especially creative, they could make a tune to match their lyrics; students do not have to use a tune that is already written.

    Sometimes it is easier to do this kind of an assignment if one has someone with whom to talk about it. Therefore, students may, if they choose, get together in small groups (2 or 3 students per group) to work on this assignment.

    Suggest that it would be a good idea for students to first stop and think about the book and Dicey's role in it -- even to jot down a few notes and ideas. From these notes, students should be able to get started with their lyrics. Students should decide what type of a song (slow, fast, happy, sad, etc.) would be best suited as Dicey's Song and then choose a melody that will be appropriate.

    Give students this class period to work on this assignment. Tell students when their "songs" will be due. If your students are creative and not too shy, it would be fun to actually schedule a performance of each of the songs by the writers!

LESSON ELEVEN

Objectives
    1. To review the main ideas and events from chapters 11-12
    2. To discuss *Dicey's Song* on interpretive and critical levels

Activity #1

    Take a few minutes at the beginning of the period to review the study questions for chapters 11-12.

Activity #2

    Choose the questions from the Extra Discussion Questions/Writing Assignments which seem most appropriate for your students. A class discussion of these questions is most effective if students have been given the opportunity to formulate answers to the questions prior to the discussion. To this end, you may either have all the students formulate answers to all the questions, divide your class into groups and assign one or more questions to each group, or you could assign one question to each student in your class. The option you choose will make a difference in the amount of class time needed for this activity. After students have had ample time to formulate answers to the questions, begin your class discussion of the questions and the ideas presented by the questions. Be sure students take notes during the discussion so they have information to study for the unit test.

EXTRA WRITING ASSIGNMENTS/DISCUSSION QUESTIONS - *Dicey's Song*

Interpretation

1. Explain how the title of the book is appropriate.

2. If you were to rewrite *Dicey's Song* as a play, where would you start and end each act? Explain why.

3. What are the main conflicts in the story? Are they resolved? If so how? If not, why not?

4. From what point of view is the story written? How does this point of view affect our understanding of the story?

5. What is the setting? How important is the setting to the story? Why?

Critical

6. Explain in what ways Dicey and Gram change during the course of the novel.

7. Are Dicey's actions believably motivated? Explain why or why not.

8. What effect does Momma's death have on Dicey? On Gram? On the themes of the story?

9. Characterize Cynthia Voigt's style of writing. How does it contribute to the value of the novel?

10. How are each of the sweater colors and Christmas presents appropriate for each of the children?

11. In discussing conflicts, Mina thought of Man versus Society, and Dicey thought of Man versus Himself. How is each of these responses appropriate to the person?

12. There are many ways one can determine the value of another person. Using the characters in this book, explain this statement.

13. Explain the relationships between Gram and Dicey, Dicey and Sammy, Dicey and Mina, James and Maybeth, and Mr. Lingerle and the Tillerman family.

14. Each of the main characters has a central problem. Explain the problems of Dicey, Gram, James, Maybeth and Sammy.

15. What function does each of the following characters serve in the novel: Mr. Lingerle, Mina, Millie, and Jeff?

Dicey's Song Extra Discussion Questions page 2

16. Are the characters in *Dicey's Song* stereotypes? If so, explain why Cynthia Voigt used stereotypes. If not, explain how the characters merit individuality.

17. What is the significance/importance of the sailboat in the novel? The wooden box? The paper mulberry tree? The Coat of Many Colors?

18. Gram has a reputation for being "crazy." Dicey calls her "crazy like a fox." What does that mean?

19. Dicey considers bravery to be an important personal trait. What kinds of bravery are shown (and by whom) in this novel?

20. Do you think the sibling relationship between Dicey and James is realistic? Explain why or why not.

21. Compare and contrast Dicey and James.

22. How and why is Maybeth special?

23. Sammy tries to be "good." Is being "good" good for Sammy? What is "good"?

24. Find all the references to song and singing in the novel and explain how each is used by the author to give substance to the story.

25. Discuss the treatment of the subjects of school and education in the novel.

26. Cynthia Voigt's characters are life-like. Look through the text and find examples of written passages which humanize her characters and make them realistic.

27. How does Dicey feel about growing up? Be specific and use examples from the text to support your statements.

28. Explain the significance of the last line of the story, "So Gram began the story."

Personal Response
25. Did you enjoy reading *Dicey's Song*? Why or why not?

26. Would you like to live in Crisfield on the Chesapeake Bay? Why or why not?

27. Who was your favorite character in the book? Why?

LESSON TWELVE

Objective
To review all of the vocabulary work done in this unit

Activity
Choose one (or more) of the vocabulary review activities listed below and spend your class period as directed in the activity. Some of the materials for these review activities are located in the Vocabulary Resource section in this unit.

VOCABULARY REVIEW ACTIVITIES

1. Divide your class into two teams and have an old-fashioned spelling or definition bee.

2. Give each of your students (or students in groups of two, three or four) a *Dicey's Song* Vocabulary Word Search Puzzle. The person (group) to find all of the vocabulary words in the puzzle first wins.

3. Give students a *Dicey's Song* Vocabulary Word Search Puzzle without the word list. The person or group to find the most vocabulary words in the puzzle wins.

4. Use a *Dicey's Song* Vocabulary Crossword Puzzle. Put the puzzle onto a transparency on the overhead projector (so everyone can see it), and do the puzzle together as a class.

5. Give students a *Dicey's Song* Vocabulary Matching Worksheet to do.

6. Divide your class into two teams. Use the *Dicey's Song* vocabulary words with their letters jumbled as a word list. Student 1 from Team A faces off against Student 1 from Team B. You write the first jumbled word on the board. The first student (1A or 1B) to unscramble the word wins the chance for his/her team to score points. If 1A wins the jumble, go to student 2A and give him/her a definition. He/she must give you the correct spelling of the vocabulary word which fits that definition. If he/she does, Team A scores a point, and you give student 3A a definition for which you expect a correctly spelled matching vocabulary word. Continue giving Team A definitions until some team member makes an incorrect response. An incorrect response sends the game back to the jumbled-word face off, this time with students 2A and 2B. Instead of repeating giving definitions to the first few students of each team, continue with the student after the one who gave the last incorrect response on the team. For example, if Team B wins the jumbled-word face-off, and student 5B gave the last incorrect answer for Team B, you would start this round of definition questions with student 6B, and so on. The team with the most points wins!

7. Have students write a story in which they correctly use as many vocabulary words as possible. Have students read their compositions orally! Post the most original compositions on your bulletin board!

LESSONS THIRTEEN AND FOURTEEN

Objectives
1. To evaluate students' project assignments
2. To give students the opportunity to practice public speaking
3. To give students a chance to show off what they have accomplished
4. To bring the project work to a close

Activity

Have students individually give their project presentations. Two class periods are allowed for this activity; you may need more or less depending on the number of students in your class, the length of your class periods, and the number of questions students have about each presentation.

LESSON FIFTEEN

Objectives
1. To give students the opportunity to practice writing to persuade
2. To give the teacher the opportunity to evaluate students' writing skills

Activity

Distribute Writing Assignment #3. Discuss the directions in detail and give students ample time to complete the assignment.

LESSON SIXTEEN

Objective

To review the main ideas presented in *Dicey's Song*

Activity #1

Choose one of the review games/activities included in this unit and spend your class period as outlined there. Some materials for these activities are located in the Unit Resource section of this unit.

Activity #2

Remind students that the Unit Test will be in the next class meeting. Stress the review of the Study Guides and their class notes as a last minute, brush-up review for homework.

WRITING ASSIGNMENT #3 - *Dicey's Song*

PROMPT

You are a marketing agent for a book publisher. The publisher has handed you *Dicey's Song* and has told you to create a one-page advertisement to be included in the book-of-the-month club mailing next month.

PREWRITING

First decide what kinds of things should go in your advertisement. You should probably include the title of the book, author's name, publisher's name, a description of what the book is about, the price of the book and a graphic relating to the book. Often quotations from book reviewers are included in book advertisements.

Decide what things will sell the book. Who is in your audience? Who will most likely purchase the book, and what about the book will most interest them? Make a list. These are the things you should use to get your readers' attention and to persuade your audience to purchase the book.

You should include a graphic. What kind of a graphic relating to the book will most appeal to your audience and will go along with (at least some of) the things on your list? Find a picture to use or draw one of your own. Photographs are also acceptable.

Make a rough layout of your ad page. Make a sketch showing your captions and the positions of your copy (words/written material) and graphic(s). You may have to do this several times before you come up with a layout (design) that you're happy with.

DRAFTING

Write out the copy (words/written material) for your ad. You may need to revise this several times before you get the wording to be as effective as possible.

After you are happy with your copy, make a mock-up (pasted-up rough draft) of your ad and see how things fit. Make any necessary corrections. For example, if your copy is too long, shorten it to fit in the space on your page. If it is too short (doesn't fill up the space you have allotted it on the page), add some to it. Fine-tune your ad until you are happy with the results.

PROMPT

When you finish the rough draft of your ad, ask a student who sits near you to look at it. After reading your rough draft, he/she should tell you what he/she liked best about your work, which parts were difficult to understand, and ways in which your work could be improved. Reread your paper considering your critic's comments, and make the corrections you think are necessary.

PROOFREADING

Do a final proofreading of your ad double-checking your grammar, spelling, organization, and the clarity of your ideas.

REVIEW GAMES/ACTIVITIES - *Dicey's Song*

1. Ask the class to make up a unit test for *Dicey's Song*. The test should have 4 sections: matching, true/false, short answer, and essay. Students may use 1/2 period to make the test and then swap papers and use the other 1/2 class period to take a test a classmate has devised. (open book) You may want to use the unit test included in this unit or take questions from the students' unit tests to formulate your own test.

2. Take 1/2 period for students to make up true and false questions (including the answers). Collect the papers and divide the class into two teams. Draw a big tic-tac-toe board on the chalk board. Make one team X and one team O. Ask questions to each side, giving each student one turn. If the question is answered correctly, that students' team's letter (X or O) is placed in the box. If the answer is incorrect, no mark is placed in the box. The object is to get three marks in a row like tic-tac-toe. You may want to keep track of the number of games won for each team.

3. Take 1/2 period for students to make up questions (true/false and short answer). Collect the questions. Divide the class into two teams. You'll alternate asking questions to individual members of teams A & B (like in a spelling bee). The question keeps going from A to B until it is correctly answered, then a new question is asked. A correct answer does not allow the team to get another question. Correct answers are +2 points; incorrect answers are -1 point.

4. Have students pair up and quiz each other from their study guides and class notes.

5. Give students a *Dicey's Song* crossword puzzle to complete.

6. Divide your class into two teams. Use the *Dicey's Song* crossword words with their letters jumbled as a word list. Student 1 from Team A faces off against Student 1 from Team B. You write the first jumbled word on the board. The first student (1A or 1B) to unscramble the word wins the chance for his/her team to score points. If 1A wins the jumble, go to student 2A and give him/her a clue. He/she must give you the correct word which matches that clue. If he/she does, Team A scores a point, and you give student 3A a clue for which you expect another correct response. Continue giving Team A clues until some team member makes an incorrect response. An incorrect response sends the game back to the jumbled-word face off, this time with students 2A and 2B. Instead of repeating giving clues to the first few students of each team, continue with the student after the one who gave the last incorrect response on the team. For example, if Team B wins the jumbled-word face-off, and student 5B gave the last incorrect answer for Team B, you would start this round of clue questions with student 6B, and so on. The team with the most points wins!

UNIT TESTS

SHORT ANSWER UNIT TEST 1 - *Dicey's Song*

I. Matching/Identify

____ 1. Maybeth   A. Wanted to help Dicey with the boat

____ 2. Gram   B. Momma's doctor

____ 3. Voigt   C. Liked to read; Dicey's brother

____ 4. Sammy   D. Played guitar after school

____ 5. Dicey   E. Store owner

____ 6. John   F. Slow learner; talented musician

____ 7. James   G. English teacher

____ 8. Jeff   H. Momma

____ 9. Mina   I. Author

____ 10. Liza   J. Music teacher

____ 11. Millie   K. Gram's husband

____ 12. Chappelle   L. Adopted the children

____ 13. Eversleigh   M. Home Ec teacher

____ 14. Lingerle   N. Dicey's school friend

                            O. Brings Tillerman children to Crisfield

Dicey's Song Short Answer Unit Test 1 Page 2

II. Short Answer

1. How does Dicey feel about school?

2. From whom and how did Dicey get a job?

3. What was Gram's response to the letter from Boston?

4. How did Dicey feel when everyone laughed at her home-ec apron?

5. How does Gram feel about getting welfare checks?

6. About what does Dicey keep nagging James?

Dicey Short Answer Unit Test 1 Page 3

7. Why did Miss Eversleigh give Dicey an F on her assignment? Why was that ironic?

8. Why did Mr. Chappelle change Dicey's grade and apologize to her?

9. What does Gram regret about her life with her own family?

10. What did Gram say to Mina's father? What did she mean?

11. Why did Gram rush up to Boston?

12. Why does Dicey feel comfortable talking about Momma to the salesman at the wood shop?

13. How did Gram react to the wood shop salesman's offering her the wooden box for free?

Dicey's Song Short Answer Unit Test 1 Page 4

III. Composition

Each of the main characters has a central problem. Explain what problem each of the following characters has, and tell if/how it is resolved: Dicey, Gram, Maybeth, James, Sammy.

Dicey's Song Short Answer Unit Test 1 Page 5

IV. Vocabulary

Listen to the vocabulary words and spell them. After you have spelled all the words, go back and write down the definitions.

1.

2.

3.

4.

5.

6.

7.

8.

9.

10.

KEY: SHORT ANSWER UNIT TEST #1 - *Dicey's Song*

I. Matching/Identify

_F_ 1. Maybeth   A. Wanted to help Dicey with the boat

_L_ 2. Gram   B. Momma's doctor

_I_ 3. Voigt   C. Liked to read; Dicey's brother

_A_ 4. Sammy   D. Played guitar after school

_O_ 5. Dicey   E. Store owner

_K_ 6. John   F. Slow learner; talented musician

_C_ 7. James   G. English teacher

_D_ 8. Jeff   H. Momma

_N_ 9. Mina   I. Author

_H_ 10. Liza   J. Music teacher

_E_ 11. Millie   K. Gram's husband

_G_ 12. Chappelle   L. Adopted the children

_M_ 13. Eversleigh   M. Home Ec teacher

_J_ 14. Lingerle   N. Dicey's school friend

                                 O. Brings Tillerman children to Crisfield

II. Short Answer

1. How does Dicey feel about school?
    She feels that "about all school was good for was using up your days."

2. From whom and how did Dicey get a job?
    Dicey went to see Millie Tydings, the woman who owned the local grocery store. She offered to clean Millie's store each afternoon. She argued that if the store were clean, Millie would have more business, which would more than pay for Dicey's work.

3. What was Gram's response to the letter from Boston?
    She decided to go ahead with the adoption of the children.

4. How did Dicey feel when everyone laughed at her home-ec apron?
    She didn't care.

5. How does Gram feel about getting welfare checks?
    She doesn't like to get them because it makes her have to let go of her pride. She would rather be self-sufficient.

6. About what does Dicey keep nagging James?
    She nags him about finding a way to teach Maybeth to read.

7. Why did Miss Eversleigh give Dicey an F on her assignment? Why was that ironic?
    Miss Eversleigh thought that no one could live long on Dicey's meals. That was ironic because in fact Dicey and the children _did_ live on those meals.

8. Why did Mr. Chappelle change Dicey's grade and apologize to her?
    He did so because Mina made him see that Dicey had not plagiarized her essay.

9. What does Gram regret about her life with her own family?
    She regrets that she never "reached out" to her own family; she just let them drift away.

10. What did Gram say to Mina's father? What did she mean?
    She said, "I've come to put a face on the bogeyman." She meant that she had come to meet them in person so they could make up their own minds about her instead of only hearing rumors about her.

11. Why did Gram rush up to Boston?
    Momma was dying, and she wanted to be with her.

12. Why does Dicey feel comfortable talking about Momma to the salesman at the wood shop?
    He seemed to genuinely care about her troubles and he sympathized with her.

13. How did Gram react to the wood shop salesman's offering her the wooden box for free?
    She was embarrassed, and she had to let go of her pride. She accepted it since it was a gift and was not out of charity.

III. Composition: Answers will vary.

IV. Vocabulary
    Choose ten of the vocabulary words. Read the words orally for students to write down.

SHORT ANSWER UNIT TEST 2 - *Dicey's Song*

I. Matching

___ 1. Maybeth   A. Played guitar after school

___ 2. Gram   B. English teacher

___ 3. Voigt   C. Adopted the children

___ 4. Sammy   D. Author

___ 5. Dicey   E. Home Ec teacher

___ 6. John   F. Music teacher

___ 7. James   G. Wanted to help Dicey with the boat

___ 8. Jeff   H. Momma

___ 9. Mina   I. Momma's doctor

___ 10. Liza   J. Slow learner; talented musician

___ 11. Millie   K. Dicey's school friend

___ 12. Chappelle   L. Liked to read; Dicey's brother

___ 13. Eversleigh   M. Store owner

___ 14. Lingerle   N. Brings Tillerman children to Crisfield

                           O. Gram's husband

Dicey's Song Short Answer Unit Test 2 page 2

II. Short Answer

1. What are the main conflicts in *Dicey's Song* and how is each resolved?

2. List three main ideas Cynthia Voigt sets forth in *Dicey's Song*.

3. Describe Mr. Lingerle's relationship with the Tillerman family.

4. In what and where was Momma buried? Why?

Dicey Short Answer Unit Test 2 Page 3

5. In what ways did Dicey change during the time of the story?

6. In *Dicey's Song* we are given many different views of education. What is one?

7. What grade did Dicey get on her report card for English? Why? Did she deserve it?

8. What does the character of Millie add to the story?

Dicey's Song Short Answer Unit Test 2 page 4

III. Composition
    Explain the significance of the phrases "hold on," "reach out," and "let go" as they relate to *Dicey's Song*.

Dicey's Song Short Answer Unit Test 2 page 5

IV. Vocabulary

    Listen to the vocabulary words and spell them. After you have spelled all the words, go back and write down the definitions.

1.

2.

3.

4.

5.

6.

7.

8.

9.

10.

KEY: SHORT ANSWER UNIT TEST 2 *Dicey's Song*

I. Matching (Use this matching key also for the Advanced Short Answer Unit Test)

_J_ 1. Maybeth	A. Played guitar after school
_C_ 2. Gram	B. English teacher
_D_ 3. Voigt	C. Adopted the children
_G_ 4. Sammy	D. Author
_N_ 5. Dicey	E. Home Ec teacher
_O_ 6. John	F. Music teacher
_L_ 7. James	G. Wanted to help Dicey with the boat
_A_ 8. Jeff	H. Momma
_K_ 9. Mina	I. Momma's doctor
_H_ 10. Liza	J. Slow learner; talented musician
_M_ 11. Millie	K. Dicey's school friend
_B_ 12. Chappelle	L. Liked to read; Dicey's brother
_E_ 13. Eversleigh	M. Store owner
_F_ 14. Lingerle	N. Brings Tillerman children to Crisfield
	O. Gram's husband

II. Short Answer: See the study guide section for answers.

III. Composition: Answers to many of these questions will depend on your class discussions and your interpretation of the story.

IV. Vocabulary: Choose ten of the vocabulary words to dictate for this section of the test.

ADVANCED SHORT ANSWER UNIT TEST - *Dicey's Song*

I. Matching

___ 1. Maybeth   A. Played guitar after school

___ 2. Gram   B. English teacher

___ 3. Voigt   C. Adopted the children

___ 4. Sammy   D. Author

___ 5. Dicey   E. Home Ec teacher

___ 6. John   F. Music teacher

___ 7. James   G. Wanted to help Dicey with the boat

___ 8. Jeff   H. Momma

___ 9. Mina   I. Momma's doctor

___ 10. Liza   J. Slow learner; talented musician

___ 11. Millie   K. Dicey's school friend

___ 12. Chappelle   L. Liked to read; Dicey's brother

___ 13. Eversleigh   M. Store owner

___ 14. Lingerle   N. Brings Tillerman children to Crisfield

                      O. Gram's husband

Dicey's Song Advanced Short Answer Unit Test Page 2

II. Short Answer

1. Explain how Dicey changes throughout the novel.

2. What effect does Momma's death have on Dicey?

3. In discussing conflicts, Mina thought of man versus society and Dicey thought of man versus himself. How is each of these responses appropriate for the character? Explain why.

4. There are many ways one can determine the value of another person. Using characters in this novel, explain this statement.

Dicey's Song Advanced Short Answer Unit Test Page 3

5. Explain the relationship between James and Maybeth.

6. What is the importance of each of the following:

   a. sailboat

   b. wooden box

   c. paper mulberry tree

7. What characteristics did Dicey's English and Home Economics teachers have in common? Give examples to support your statements.

Dicey's Song Advanced Short Answer Unit Test page 4

III. Composition

    Discuss the theme/idea of communication as it relates to *Dicey's Song*.

Dicey's Song Advanced Short Answer Unit Test page 5

IV. Vocabulary

Listen to the vocabulary words and write them down. After you have written down all the words, write a paragraph using all of the vocabulary words. The paragraph must in some way relate to *Dicey's Song*.

MULTIPLE CHOICE UNIT TEST 1 - *Dicey's Song*

I. Matching

____ 1. Maybeth   A. Wanted to help Dicey with the boat

____ 2. Gram   B. Momma's doctor

____ 3. Voigt   C. Liked to read; Dicey's brother

____ 4. Sammy   D. Played guitar after school

____ 5. Dicey   E. Store owner

____ 6. John   F. Slow learner; talented musician

____ 7. James   G. English teacher

____ 8. Jeff   H. Momma

____ 9. Mina   I. Author

____ 10. Liza   J. Music teacher

____ 11. Millie   K. Gram's husband

____ 12. Chappelle   L. Adopted the children

____ 13. Eversleigh   M. Home Ec teacher

____ 14. Lingerle   N. Dicey's school friend

                                     O. Brings Tillerman children to Crisfield

Dicey's Song Multiple Choice Unit Test 1 Page 2

II. Multiple Choice

1. How does Dicey feel about school?
    a. She thinks it is very interesting.
    b. She thinks all it does is use up the days.
    c. She hates it.
    d. She enjoys science, but dislikes all the other subjects.

2. How did Dicey convince Millie Tydings to give her a job?
    a. She told her that if the store were cleaner she would have more business.
    b. She told her what a good worker she would be, and that she would work for less than minimum wage.
    c. She said she would also clean Millie's house for free every week.
    d. She told her that her brothers would also come and help for free.

3. Why does Millie always make mistakes on the order forms?
    a. She needs glasses but refuses to get them.
    b. She has a drinking problem which affects her vision.
    c. She cannot read.
    d. She is always trying to do more than one thing at a time and doesn't pay attention to what she is doing.

4. About whom does Dicey write her English composition?
    a. Momma
    b. Jeff
    c. Sammy and Maybeth
    d. Will Hawkins

5. What is Maybeth's problem in school?
    a. She refuses to do any work.
    b. She is so far ahead that she is bored and is becoming a behavior problem.
    c. She works hard but does not make any progress.
    d. She cries all of the time and can't seem to concentrate on her work.

6. About what does Dicey keep nagging James?
    a. Helping her find a boyfriend
    b. Brushing his teeth and keeping himself clean
    c. Doing his household chores
    d. Teaching Maybeth to read

Dicey Multiple Choice Unit Test 1 Page 3

7. What does Dicey think of her report card grade in English?
    a. She thinks it must be a mistake.
    b. She thinks it is a fair grade.
    c. She thinks her teacher is just trying to make her work harder.
    d. She doesn't care about the grade at all; she thinks school is useless, anyway, and doesn't care whether she gets good grades or not.

8. Of what does Mr. Chappelle accuse Dicey?
    a. Plagiarism
    b. Slander
    c. Conspiracy
    d. Bribery

9. How do Gram and Dicey afford to go to Boston?
    a. They take in cleaning and sewing to make the extra money.
    b. They ask the pastor of their church to help them out.
    c. They skimp on food to save money.
    d. Gram sells a spoon.

10. Does Dicey feel comfortable talking to the salesman at the wood shop?
    a. Yes, it is easy to talk to him because he is a stranger.
    b. Yes, he reminds her of her father.
    c. No, he is a rather stiff and stern man.
    d. No, she is a little scared of him.

11. How does Gram react to the wood shop salesman's offer to give her the wooden box for free?
    a. She lets go of her pride and accepts it as a gift, not charity.
    b. She becomes proud and stubborn and refuses it.
    c. She breaks down into tears at such a beautiful, thoughtful gesture.
    d. She recognizes that it is charity and accepts it, but she feels disappointed in herself and becomes depressed.

12. Which is not a main conflict in *Dicey's Song*?
    a. Man versus man
    b. Man versus himself
    c. Man versus society
    d. Man versus nature

Dicey's Song Multiple Choice Unit Test 1 Page 4

III. Composition - Answer in complete paragraphs.

1. In what ways did Dicey change throughout the novel?

2. Each of the main characters has a central problem in the novel. Explain Dicey's problem(s).

3. What effect did Momma's death have on Dicey?

Dicey's Song Multiple Choice Unit Test 1 Page 5

IV. Vocabulary: Multiple choice. Write in the letter of the word that matches the definition.

____ 1. HARRIED		A. Loaded; burdened
____ 2. SYMMETRICAL		B. Liable to fall or break down because of weakness
____ 3. LAPEL		C. A special quality that inspires allegiance and devotion
____ 4. CHARISMA		D. Subdued; restrained from excess
____ 5. RICKETY		E. A radiance encircling the head or body; a halo
____ 6. LINGERED		F. To declare firmly and persistently
____ 7. TENDENCY		G. Expect the best outcome
____ 8. OPTIMISTIC		H. Rolling, pitching or swaying suddenly
____ 9. WARY		I. Exact correspondence of form on opposite sides of a dividing line
____ 10. LADEN		J. Cautious
____ 11. REVERBERATED		K. Continued to stay; delayed; loitered
____ 12. DECEITFULNESS		L. A slow, stately dance or music for such a dance
____ 13. AUREOLE		M. Dishonest action or trick; fraud or lie
____ 14. CHASTENED		N. To be reflected as light or sound waves
____ 15. MINSTREL		O. Intense or eager interest; passion
____ 16. MANNIKINS		P. Models of the human body usually used in stores
____ 17. ENTHUSIASM		Q. A travelling poet, singer or musician
____ 18. MINUET		R. Inclination to move or act in a particular way
____ 19. LURCHING		S. Part of a jacket folded back from the neckline
____ 20. INSISTED		T. Tormented or worried; harassed

MULTIPLE CHOICE UNIT TEST 2 - *Dicey's Song*

I. Matching

___ 1. Maybeth   A. Played guitar after school

___ 2. Gram   B. English teacher

___ 3. Voigt   C. Adopted the children

___ 4. Sammy   D. Author

___ 5. Dicey   E. Home Ec teacher

___ 6. John   F. Music teacher

___ 7. James   G. Wanted to help Dicey with the boat

___ 8. Jeff   H. Momma

___ 9. Mina   I. Momma's doctor

___ 10. Liza   J. Slow learner; talented musician

___ 11. Millie   K. Dicey's school friend

___ 12. Chappelle   L. Liked to read; Dicey's brother

___ 13. Eversleigh   M. Store owner

___ 14. Lingerle   N. Brings Tillerman children to Crisfield

                                    O. Gram's husband

Dicey's Song Multiple Choice Unit Test 2 Page 2

II. Multiple Choice

1. How does Dicey feel about school?
    a. She hates it.
    b. She thinks it is very interesting.
    c. She thinks all it does is use up the days.
    d. She enjoys science, but dislikes all the other subjects.

2. How did Dicey convince Millie Tydings to give her a job?
    a. She told her what a good worker she would be, and that she would work for less than minimum wage.
    b. She told her that if the store were cleaner she would have more business.
    c. She told her that her brothers would also come and help for free.
    d. She said she would also clean Millie's house for free every week.

3. Why does Millie always make mistakes on the order forms?
    a. She is always trying to do more than one thing at a time and doesn't pay attention to what she is doing.
    b. She has a drinking problem which affects her vision.
    c. She needs glasses but refuses to get them.
    d. She cannot read.

4. About whom does Dicey write her English composition?
    a. Sammy and Maybeth
    b. Will Hawkins
    c. Momma
    d. Jeff

5. What is Maybeth's problem in school?
    a. She works hard but does not make any progress.
    b. She cries all of the time and can't seem to concentrate on her work.
    c. She refuses to do any work.
    d. She is so far ahead that she is bored and is becoming a behavior problem.

6. About what does Dicey keep nagging James?
    a. Helping her find a boyfriend
    b. Teaching Maybeth to read
    c. Brushing his teeth and keeping himself clean
    d. Doing his household chores

Dicey Multiple Choice Unit Test 2 Page 3

7. What does Dicey think of her report card grade in English?
    a. She thinks her teacher is just trying to make her work harder.
    b. She doesn't care about the grade at all; she thinks school is useless, anyway, and doesn't care whether she gets good grades or not.
    c. She thinks it must be a mistake.
    d. She thinks it is a fair grade.

8. Of what does Mr. Chappelle accuse Dicey?
    a. Slander
    b. Bribery
    c. Conspiracy
    d. Plagiarism

9. How do Gram and Dicey afford to go to Boston?
    a. Gram sells a spoon.
    b. They take in cleaning and sewing to make the extra money.
    c. They skimp on food to save money.
    d. They ask the pastor of their church to help them out.

10. Does Dicey feel comfortable talking to the salesman at the wood shop?
    a. No, she is a little scared of him.
    b. Yes, it is easy to talk to him because he is a stranger.
    c. No, he is a rather stiff and stern man.
    d. Yes, he reminds her of her father.

11. How does Gram react to the wood shop salesman's offer to give her the wooden box for free?
    a. She recognizes that it is charity and accepts it, but she feels disappointed in herself and becomes depressed.
    b. She breaks down into tears at such a beautiful, thoughtful gesture.
    c. She becomes proud and stubborn and refuses it.
    d. She lets go of her pride and accepts it as a gift, not charity.

12. Which is not a main conflict in *Dicey's Song*?
    a. Man versus nature
    b. Man versus society
    c. Man versus man
    d. Man versus himself

Dicey's Song Multiple Choice Unit Test 2 Page 4

III. Composition

The Fawcett Juniper edition of *Dicey's Song* said, ". . . Slowly Dicey begins to understand that *everyone* has something to teach and that life is a lesson that doesn't get easier. . . ."

Defend this statement using specific examples from the book.

Dicey's Song Multiple Choice Unit Test 2 Page 5

IV. Vocabulary: Multiple choice. Write in the letter of the word that matches the definition.

_____ 1. CREMATED   A. Liable to fall or break down because of weakness

_____ 2. REVERBERATED   B. Easy to do, use, or get to

_____ 3. TRIUMPHANTLY   C. Continued to stay; delayed; loitered

_____ 4. MANNIKINS   D. Not sharp or certain; hazily

_____ 5. CONVENIENT   E. Tormented or worried; harassed

_____ 6. MINSTREL   F. Write or speak easily, smoothly and expressively

_____ 7. TENDENCY   G. Coagulated; solidified or thickened

_____ 8. AUREOLE   H. Burnt up; burned a dead body to ashes

_____ 9. SYMMETRICAL   I. Particularly; exactly

_____ 10. ANTICIPATING   J. Inclination to move or act in a particular way

_____ 11. CHARISMA   K. A radiance encircling the head or body; a halo

_____ 12. LAPEL   L. To be reflected as light or sound waves

_____ 13. RICKETY   M. Oppose verbally; go against; assert the opposite

_____ 14. LINGERED   N. Exact correspondence of form on opposite sides of a dividing line

_____ 15. CONGEALED   O. A special quality that inspires allegiance and devotion

_____ 16. CONTRADICT   P. Part of a jacket folded back from the neckline

_____ 17. PRECISELY   Q. Models of the human body usually used in stores

_____ 18. FLUENTLY   R. Successfully; elated

_____ 19. HARRIED   S. A travelling poet, singer or musician

_____ 20. VAGUELY   T. Looking forward to or expecting

MULTIPLE CHOICE UNIT TESTS ANSWER SHEET - *Dicey's Song*

I. Matching	II. Multiple Choice	IV. Vocabulary
1. ___	1. ___	1. ___
2. ___	2. ___	2. ___
3. ___	3. ___	3. ___
4. ___	4. ___	4. ___
5. ___	5. ___	5. ___
6. ___	6. ___	6. ___
7. ___	7. ___	7. ___
8. ___	8. ___	8. ___
9. ___	9. ___	9. ___
10. ___	10. ___	10. ___
11. ___	11. ___	11. ___
12. ___	12. ___	12. ___
13. ___		13. ___
14. ___		14. ___
		15. ___
		16. ___
		17. ___
		18. ___
		19. ___
		20. ___

ANSWER KEY - *Dicey's Song*
Multiple Choice Unit Tests

Answers to Unit Test 1 are in the left column. Answers to Unit Test 2 are in the right column.

I. Matching	II. Multiple Choice	IV. Vocabulary
1. F J	1. B C	1. T H
2. L C	2. A B	2. I L
3. I D	3. C D	3. S R
4. A G	4. A C	4. C Q
5. O N	5. C A	5. B B
6. K O	6. D B	6. K S
7. C L	7. A C	7. R J
8. D A	8. A D	8. G K
9. N K	9. D A	9. J N
10. H H	10. A B	10. A T
11. E M	11. A D	11. N O
12. G B	12. D A	12. M P
13. M E		13. E A
14. J F		14. D C
		15. Q G
		16. P M
		17. O I
		18. L F
		19. H E
		20. F D

UNIT RESOURCE MATERIALS

BULLETIN BOARD IDEAS - *Dicey's Song*

1. Save one corner of the board for the best of students' *Dicey's Song* writing assignments.

2. Title the board DICEY'S SONG with a line of written music on either side of the title and post quotes from the novel.

3. As an introductory activity have students bring in lyrics from popular ballads and post them. (The lyrics should tell a story.)

4. Take one of the word search puzzles from the extra activities section and with a marker copy it over in a large size on the bulletin board. Write the clue words to find to one side. Invite students prior to and after class to find the words and circle them on the bulletin board.

5. Post a map of Maryland showing the Chesapeake Bay, Crisfield, and Salisbury. Post pictures of things related to the bay (crabs, rockfish, skipjacks/sailboats, watermen working, the Chesapeake Bay Bridge, etc.).

6. Make a bulletin board listing the vocabulary words for this unit. As you complete sections of the novel and discuss the vocabulary for each section, write the definitions on the bulletin board. (If your board is one students face frequently, it will help them learn the words.)

7. Make a family tree for the Tillermans to show the relationships among the generations mentioned.

8. Make a bulletin board about reading -- tips for improving reading skills.

9. Make a bulletin board about home economics -- practical information about how to economically run a household.

EXTRA ACTIVITIES - *Dicey's Song*

One of the difficulties in teaching a novel is that all students don't read at the same speed. One student who likes to read may take the book home and finish it in a day or two. Sometimes a few students finish the in-class assignments early. The problem, then, is finding suitable extra activities for students.

One thing you can do is to keep a little library in the classroom. For this unit on *Dicey's Song*, you might check out from the school library other related books and articles about adoption, the Chesapeake Bay, sailing/boating, our welfare system, nutrition, our education system, improving one's reading, or institutions. "How to" books would be good to have on hand for students to look through for projects.

Other things you may keep on hand are puzzles. We have made some relating directly to *Dicey's Song* for you. Feel free to duplicate them.

Some students may like to draw. You might devise a contest or allow some extra-credit grade for students who draw characters or scenes from *Dicey's Song*. Note, too, that if the students do not want to keep their drawings you may pick up some extra bulletin board materials this way. If you have a contest and you supply the prize (a CD or something like that perhaps), you could, possibly, make the drawing itself a non-refundable entry fee.

The pages which follow contain games, puzzles and worksheets. The keys, when appropriate, immediately follow the puzzle or worksheet. There are two main groups of activities: one group for the unit; that is, generally relating to the *Dicey's Song* text, and another group of activities related strictly to the *Dicey's Song* vocabulary.

Directions for these games, puzzles and worksheets are self-explanatory. The object here is to provide you with extra materials you may use in any way you choose.

MORE ACTIVITIES - *Dicey's Song*

1. Pick a chapter or scene with a great deal of dialogue and have the students act it out on a stage. (Perhaps you could assign various scenes to different groups of students so more than one scene could be acted and more students could participate.)

2. Use some of the related topics (noted earlier for an in-class library) as topics for research, reports or written papers, or as topics for guest speakers.

3. Spend a day showing students tips about how to improve reading skills.

4. Have students design a book cover (front and back and inside flaps) for *Dicey's Song*.

5. Have students design a bulletin board (ready to be put up; not just sketched) for Dicey's Song.

6. Have a Maryland Day during which you learn about the state of Maryland.

7. Have students choose one chapter of the book (with sufficient dialogue) to rewrite as a play. In conjunction with this assignment, have students write a composition explaining the difficulties they encountered in changing from one written form to another.

8. Have students write their own "songs." (For example, "Judy's Song," "Ben's Song," "Tonya's Song," etc.). The lyrics for their songs should relate to their own personal lives.

9. Discuss family traditions -- things your students' families do for holidays, birthdays, vacations, or any time they do something special that is a tradition.

10. Do a mini-unit on home economics giving students tips about running a cost-effective home.

WORD SEARCH - *Dicey's Song*

All words in this list are associated with *Dicey's Song*. The words are placed backwards, forward, diagonally, up and down. The included words are listed below the word search.

```
W E L F A R E N A L I N G E R L E V Y D L V T T
Q W Q N D X B S G D F Q Z X L C T E C T Y W W M
C C C M X D B L T M O D Q G J L N P S G W B D R
E V E R S L E I G H L P N Y N O E F K C X X S B
D K N D C Z L M G E P I T Y M X N P T H X V X J
G W V H J K V M I G G Z C I T G T J P Q M S V R
G R K L V H H F W G G J G G O H R F W A Y G Q W
Y G X M J T S M E G L P R J T N I Y F C H Q T R
M Q F F E I D L C S D W W J J R T R T P Y C P J
T H Q B R L T H K M N I Y T O X M H T H G G W L
M A Y C M O D V Y D S W C C A X W B G E K Y S M
S A O W O U Y A H Q A H K E V O X D B I E J X C
M A R B L E S M U L B E R R Y B B O X H O N K Y
G I N G L S L I M C T H R R F P M N N H O V C H
Z U L O E I G W C A M Z E Y F I D A N T Q Z R Y
A Z I L T T A F Y N S C I E N C E S J T V L R
W P P T I E F S Z P O E I A F C F O L A A E C H
T N R M A E W Q O R D P V T O V B T F R G M N L
L V Q O J R T O G H N Y Z E T L C B D N Z P E P
K V N D N H N J K P P Z N V N A D Y A X H P L S
```

ADOPTION	ESSAY	LIZA	ROCKET
ANGEL	EVERSLEIGH	MARBLES	SAILBOAT
APRON	FAT	MAYBETH	SAMMY
ATTIC	GRAM	MILLIE	SCIENCE
BOAT	GROCERY	MINA	SEVEN
BOOTLEGGING	GUITAR	MONEY	SPOON
BOSTON	HONKY	MULBERRY	TEN
BOX	JAMES	MUSIC	THIRTEEN
CHAPPELLE	JEFF	NOTE	VOIGT
CRISFIELD	JOHN	OCEAN	WELFARE
DICEY	LINGERLE	READ	

KEY: WORD SEARCH - *Dicey's Song*

All words in this list are associated with *Dicey's Song*. The words are placed backwards, forward, diagonally, up and down. The included words are listed below the word search.

```
    W E L F A R E     A L I N G E R L E   Y
                      D           L       E
                    O D   G       L N
    E V E R S L E I G H L P N     O E
                      E   I T         P
                    I   G     I T         P
                  H F   G             O H       A
                T S   E                 N I         H
              E I   L     D               R T R         C
    T     B R   T       I   T O             H T
    M A Y C M O       Y D     C C A           G E
      A O   O U Y A         A   K E O           I E J
    M A R B L E S M U L B E R R Y     B O X H O N K Y
    G I N G L S     I M     T   R R       M   N H O V
      U L O E I         C A       E       I   A N T
    A Z I L T     A F     S C I E N C E   S J T     L
        P   T I E F S   P O E I A   C     O   A A E
          R   A E     O R     V T O     B   F   G M N
            O J R   O G         E T             N   E
              N   N                 N A           A     S
```

ADOPTION	ESSAY	LIZA	ROCKET
ANGEL	EVERSLEIGH	MARBLES	SAILBOAT
APRON	FAT	MAYBETH	SAMMY
ATTIC	GRAM	MILLIE	SCIENCE
BOAT	GROCERY	MINA	SEVEN
BOOTLEGGING	GUITAR	MONEY	SPOON
BOSTON	HONKY	MULBERRY	TEN
BOX	JAMES	MUSIC	THIRTEEN
CHAPPELLE	JEFF	NOTE	VOIGT
CRISFIELD	JOHN	OCEAN	WELFARE
DICEY	LINGERLE	READ	

CROSSWORD - *Dicey's Song*

CROSSWORD CLUES - *Dicey's Song*

ACROSS

2. Liked to read; Dicey's brother
5. Author
9. Brings the Tillerman children to Crisfield.
11. Gram's transportation downtown
12. Store owner
14. Everyone laughed at Dicey's ___; her home-ec creation
16. Slow learner; talented musician
20. Dicey says Maybeth looks like a Christmas ___
23. Mr. Lingerle's physical condition
25. A single
26. Opposite of noisy
27. Crisfield or Salisbury, for example
28. Mina's friends called Dicey this name
31. Sammy's age
32. Played guitar after school
34. Home Ec teacher
36. Negative reply
37. Mr. Lingerle gave Gram an envelope with ___ in it
38. Dicey and Wilhemina worked together on a ___ project
41. Dicey bought Sammy a toy ___
44. Have the same opinion
47. Gram gets these checks
48. Presents
49. City where Momma was staying
50. Gram sells it to get money to go to Boston
51. They buried Momma under the paper ___ tree.

DOWN

1. Process by which Gram became guardian of the children
2. Gram's husband
3. Dicey's school friend
4. Wanted to help Dicey with the boat
6. Dicey's conversations with Mina were 'like running along the ---'
7. Adopted the children
8. Dicey had one from the music teacher requesting a conference
10. English teacher
13. Momma
15. Dicey wanted James to find a way to help Maybeth ___
17. The children got into trouble looking at things in Gram's ___
18. Former illegal profession of the Tillmans
19. Dicey's age at the beginning of the book
21. Millie owned a ___ store
22. Music teacher
24. James's age
29. Indebted to; to --- someone a favor
30. Mr. Chappelle accused Dicey of plagiarizing her ___
33. Device used to move air
35. Jeff's instrument
37. Gram won these from the second graders
38. Dicey's pot of gold
39. Town where Dicey lives
40. Myself
42. Waxy coloring instrument kids use
43. Looking at
45. People who read
46. Maybeth's talent
49. The man at the wood store gave Dicey a ___

CROSSWORD ANSWER KEY - *Dicey's Song*

MATCHING QUIZ/WORKSHEET 1 - *Dicey's Song*

____ 1. ATTIC   A. Jeff's instrument

____ 2. CHAPPELLE   B. Gram's husband

____ 3. MUSIC   C. Mina's friends called Dicey this name

____ 4. GUITAR   D. Author

____ 5. LIZA   E. The children got into trouble looking at things in Gram's ___

____ 6. VOIGT   F. English teacher

____ 7. SPOON   G. Maybeth's talent

____ 8. BOSTON   H. Everyone laughed at Dicey's ___; her home-ec creation

____ 9. THIRTEEN   I. Dicey's pot of gold

____ 10. GROCERY   J. Liked to read; Dicey's brother

____ 11. APRON   K. They buried Momma under the paper ___ tree

____ 12. JAMES   L. Dicey's conversations with Mina were 'like running along the ---'

____ 13. ESSAY   M. Dicey's age at the beginning of the book

____ 14. SAILBOAT   N. City where Momma was staying

____ 15. HONKY   O. Gram sells it to get money to go to Boston

____ 16. MULBERRY   P. Adopted the children

____ 17. JOHN   Q. Momma

____ 18. GRAM   R. Slow learner; talented musician

____ 19. MAYBETH   S. Mr. Chappelle accused Dicey of plagiarizing her ___

____ 20. OCEAN   T. Millie owned a ____ store

KEY: MATCHING QUIZ/WORKSHEET 1 - *Dicey's Song*

__E_ 1. ATTIC   A. Jeff's instrument

__F_ 2. CHAPPELLE   B. Gram's husband

__G_ 3. MUSIC   C. Mina's friends called Dicey this name

__A_ 4. GUITAR   D. Author

__Q_ 5. LIZA   E. The children got into trouble looking at things in Gram's

__D_ 6. VOIGT   F. English teacher

__O_ 7. SPOON   G. Maybeth's talent

__N_ 8. BOSTON   H. Everyone laughed at Dicey's ___; her home-ec creation

__M_ 9. THIRTEEN   I. Dicey's pot of gold

__T_ 10. GROCERY   J. Liked to read; Dicey's brother

__H_ 11. APRON   K. They buried Momma under the paper ___ tree

__J_ 12. JAMES   L. Dicey's conversations with Mina were 'like running along the ---'

__S_ 13. ESSAY   M. Dicey's age at the beginning of the book

__I_ 14. SAILBOAT   N. City where Momma was staying

__C_ 15. HONKY   O. Gram sells it to get money to go to Boston

__K_ 16. MULBERRY   P. Adopted the children

__B_ 17. JOHN   Q. Momma

__P_ 18. GRAM   R. Slow learner; talented musician

__R_ 19. MAYBETH   S. Mr. Chappelle accused Dicey of plagiarizing her ___

__L_ 20. OCEAN   T. Millie owned a ____ store

MATCHING QUIZ/WORKSHEET 2 - *Dicey's Song*

____ 1. ROCKET   A. Adopted the children

____ 2. SAMMY   B. Wanted to help Dicey with the boat

____ 3. LIZA   C. Gram gets these checks

____ 4. ESSAY   D. Liked to read; Dicey's brother

____ 5. WELFARE   E. Dicey bought Sammy a toy ---

____ 6. OCEAN   F. Dicey's conversations with Mina were 'like running along the ---'

____ 7. BOSTON   G. Mina's friends called Dicey this name

____ 8. MILLIE   H. Mr. Chappelle accused Dicey of plagiarizing her ___

____ 9. SCIENCE   I. Dicey wanted James to find a way to help Maybeth ___

____ 10. SAILBOAT   J. The children got into trouble looking at things in Gram's ___

____ 11. READ   K. Gram's husband

____ 12. MONEY   L. Gram sells it to get money to go to Boston

____ 13. JOHN   M. City where Momma was staying

____ 14. SPOON   N. Dicey and Wilhemina worked together on a ___ project

____ 15. NOTE   O. Momma

____ 16. ATTIC   P. Dicey's pot of gold

____ 17. SEVEN   Q. Sammy's age

____ 18. HONKY   R. Mr. Lingerle gave Gram an envelope with ___ in it

____ 19. GRAM   S. Dicey had one from the music teacher requesting a conference

____ 20. JAMES   T. Store owner

KEY: MATCHING QUIZ/WORKSHEET 2 - *Dicey's Song*

__E_ 1. ROCKET   A. Adopted the children

__B_ 2. SAMMY   B. Wanted to help Dicey with the boat

__O_ 3. LIZA   C. Gram gets these checks

__H_ 4. ESSAY   D. Liked to read; Dicey's brother

__C_ 5. WELFARE   E. Dicey bought Sammy a toy ---

__F_ 6. OCEAN   F. Dicey's conversations with Mina were 'like running along the ---'

__M_ 7. BOSTON   G. Mina's friends called Dicey this name

__T_ 8. MILLIE   H. Mr. Chappelle accused Dicey of plagiarizing her ___

__N_ 9. SCIENCE   I. Dicey wanted James to find a way to help Maybeth ___

__P_ 10. SAILBOAT   J. The children got into trouble looking at things in Gram's ___

__I_ 11. READ   K. Gram's husband

__R_ 12. MONEY   L. Gram sells it to get money to go to Boston

__K_ 13. JOHN   M. City where Momma was staying

__L_ 14. SPOON   N. Dicey and Wilhemina worked together on a ___ project

__S_ 15. NOTE   O. Momma

__J_ 16. ATTIC   P. Dicey's pot of gold

__Q_ 17. SEVEN   Q. Sammy's age

__G_ 18. HONKY   R. Mr. Lingerle gave Gram an envelope with ___ in it

__A_ 19. GRAM   S. Dicey had one from the music teacher requesting a conference

__D_ 20. JAMES   T. Store owner

JUGGLE LETTER REVIEW GAME CLUE SHEET - *Dicey's Song*

SCRAMBLED	WORD	CLUE
THEBAYM	MAYBETH	Slow learner; talented musician
MARG	GRAM	Adopted the children
TOVIG	VOIGT	Author
YAMMS	SAMMY	Wanted to help Dicey with the boat
YICED	DICEY	Brings the Tillerman children to Crisfield
HONJ	JOHN	Gram's husband
SAJEM	JAMES	Liked to read; Dicey's brother
FEJF	JEFF	Played guitar after school
INAM	MINA	Dicey's school friend
ZILA	LIZA	Momma
ILEMIL	MILLIE	Store owner
HAPPLECLE	CHAPPELLE	English teacher
SHEEVIGLER	EVERSLEIGH	Home Ec teacher
GLINEERL	LINGERLE	Music teacher
TAF	FAT	Mr. Lingerle's physical condition
ONRAP	APRON	Everyone laughed at Dicey's ___; her home-ec creation
FELAREW	WELFARE	Gram gets these checks
TACIT	ATTIC	The children got into trouble looking at things in Gram's ___
YNOKH	HONKY	Mina's friends called Dicey this name
DEAR	READ	Dicey wanted James to find a way to help Maybeth
YESAS	ESSAY	Mr. Chappelle accused Dicey of plagiarizing her ___
INGLOOTGEBG	BOOTLEGGING	Former illegal profession of the Tillermans
ANCEO	OCEAN	Dicey's conversations with Mina were 'like running along the ---'
EBLARMS	MARBLES	Gram won these from the second graders
ABLATOSI	SAILBOAT	Dicey's pot of gold
HETTERNI	THIRTEEN	Dicey's age at the beginning of the book
TOAB	BOAT	Gram's transportation downtown
NET	TEN	James's age
VEENS	SEVEN	Sammy's age
GLANE	ANGEL	Dicey says Maybeth looks like a Christmas ___
REYORGC	GROCERY	Millie owned a ____ store
RESLIDFIC	CRISFIELD	Town where Dicey lives

TONE	NOTE	Dicey had one from the music teacher requesting a conference
ENSICCE	SCIENCE	Dicey and Wilhemina worked together on a ___ project
NOTOBS	BOSTON	City where Momma was staying
INTAPOOD	ADOPTION	Process by which Gram became guardian of the children
RUTIGA	GUITAR	Jeff's instrument
SCUMI	MUSIC	Maybeth's talent
POSON	SPOON	Gram sells it to get money to go to Boston
MOYEN	MONEY	Mr. Lingerle gave Gram an envelope with ___ in it
TRECKO	ROCKET	Dicey bought Sammy a toy ---
XOB	BOX	The man at the wood store gave Dicey a ___
RUMYBLER	MULBERRY	They buried Momma under the paper ___ tree

VOCABULARY RESOURCE MATERIALS

VOCABULARY WORD SEARCH - *Dicey's Song*

All words in this list are associated with *Dicey's Song* with an emphasis on the vocabulary words chosen for study in the text. The words are placed backwards, forward, diagonally, up and down. The included words are listed below.

```
T S C Z N L J Q Y Q V E K Z T M E H W D T X D Y
J N S G L R A G R C L L N E E A M P A C W Q P
R P E E N K B P B O P D P R O P N N A O R V G S
D I M I N I S H E D E R E G N I L D N N N Y U T
G S C E N L R R F L E F E I P L S F E I A L X G
G L D K Z E U E F L R T D C R R E U G N K T N W
S A X O E A V F D E U B S D I R E J R Y C I E B
L G N S P T X N T N I E A I E S A C S T H Y N L
T A X T E T Y N O I A H N L S D I H I C N H G S
C M C U I D I C C C E E C T M N N O R S Q I G Y
D R N I H C E M O H V C M S L Y I U N Q E F S D
P I E J R H I N I N A A E I I Y L Q O X S L N K
M K W M Q T T P E S G R G D N M H L F F T V Y T
X Z K D A R E N A T T E I U J S K Z L P B N G C
S T D F A T T M M T S I A S E B T K H V N M Z T
V L Y D J K E B M G I A C L M L W R Z H T R U V
B N I F R W K D X Y H N H C E A Y Q E M Z T R D
G C E N T H U S I A S M G C G D B T N L J L L W
T Y P T N R W P J R P P Q D S G S C K K Z G L S
R E V E R B E R A T E D T R I U M P H A N T L Y
```

ANTICIPATING	DECEITFULNESS	LADEN	PRECISELY
AUREOLE	DIMINISHED	LAPEL	PRECISION
BALMY	DUMBFOUNDED	LINGERED	REVERBERATED
CHARISMA	EMANATE	LURCHING	RICKETY
CHASTENED	ENTHUSIASM	MANNIKINS	SULKY
CONFER	FLUENTLY	MEANDERING	SYMMETRICAL
CONGEALED	HARRIED	MINSTREL	TENDENCY
CONTRADICT	INSISTED	MINUET	TRIUMPHANTLY
CONVENIENT	INTERFERE	MISCHIEF	VAGUELY
CREMATED	INTRUSION	OPTIMISTIC	WARY

KEY: VOCABULARY WORD SEARCH - *Dicey's Song*

All words in this list are associated with *Dicey's Song* with an emphasis on the vocabulary words chosen for study in the text. The words are placed backwards, forward, diagonally, up and down. The included words are listed below.

```
        T   S           L                   E           T   M   E
          N S G       A           L           N E E A M       A C
          R   E   E   N       P       O P D       R O       N N A O R                   S
          D I M I N I S H E D E R E G N I L D N N               Y U
                C E N L R R F L E F E I P       S F E I A L                   G
                D K   E U E F L R T       C R R E U       N K T N
          A       O E A V F D E U B S D I R E       R Y C I E
      L       N       P T   N T N I E A I E S A C       T H Y N
              A   T E T Y N O I A H N L S D I H I C N                         S
      C   C U I D I C C C E E C T M N N O R S           I
          R N I   C E M O H V C M S L Y I U N           E
          I E   R   I N I N A A E I I Y L O           L
  M           M   T T P E S G R G D N M           F                       Y
                  A R E   A T T E I U       S               B
                    A T   M   T S I A S E       T               M
                      D   E   M   I A C L M L       R                           U
                  I       D   Y   N H   E A Y   E                           D
                  C E N T H U S I A S M G C       D                 L
  T
  T R E V E R B E R A T E D T R I U M P H A N T L Y
```

ANTICIPATING	DECEITFULNESS	LADEN	PRECISELY
AUREOLE	DIMINISHED	LAPEL	PRECISION
BALMY	DUMBFOUNDED	LINGERED	REVERBERATED
CHARISMA	EMANATE	LURCHING	RICKETY
CHASTENED	ENTHUSIASM	MANNIKINS	SULKY
CONFER	FLUENTLY	MEANDERING	SYMMETRICAL
CONGEALED	HARRIED	MINSTREL	TENDENCY
CONTRADICT	INSISTED	MINUET	TRIUMPHANTLY
CONVENIENT	INTERFERE	MISCHIEF	VAGUELY
CREMATED	INTRUSION	OPTIMISTIC	WARY

VOCABULARY CROSSWORD - *Dicey's Song*

VOCABULARY CROSSWORD CLUES - *Dicey's Song*

ACROSS
1. Burnt up; burned a dead body to ashes
7. Made smaller; lessened; reduced
10. To have a conference or talk
11. Dicey had one from the music teacher requesting a conference
13. Easy to do, use, or get to
16. Dicey's conversations with Mina were 'like running along the ---'
17. Slang for child
18. Attempt
19. Mr. Lingerle's physical condition
20. Adopted the children
21. A radiance encircling the head or body; a halo
23. Amusing
24. Grassy area; yard
25. Present plural of 'to be'
26. Tormented or worried; harassed
30. A special quality that inspires allegiance and devotion
32. To be reflected as light or sound waves
33. Loaded; burdened
34. Intense or eager interest; passion
37. Sammy's age
38. Looking forward to or expecting
40. Write or speak easily, smoothly and expressively
42. Continued to stay; delayed; loitered
44. Brings the Tillerman children to Crisfield
45. Dicey wanted James to find a way to help Maybeth ___
46. Dicey and Wilhemina worked together on a ___ project

DOWN
2. A slow, stately dance or music for such a dance
3. Definite article
4. Dicey's school friend
5. To declare firmly and persistently
6. An aimless wandering; rambling
7. Dishonest action or trick; fraud or lie
8. Models of the human body usually used in stores
9. Showing resentment and ill humor
10. Coagulated; solidified or thickened
12. Wanted to help Dicey with the boat
13. Oppose verbally; go against; assert the opposite
14. Purely bad
15. James's age
22. To flow out; come forth; emit
24. Part of a jacket folded back from the neckline
27. Town where Dicey lives
28. Not sharp or certain; hazily
29. Inclination to move or act in a particular way
30. Subdued; restrained from excess
31. A travelling poet, singer or musician
35. Soothing; mild; pleasant
36. Opposite of closed
39. The children got into trouble looking at things in Gram's ___
41. Momma
43. Frozen water

VOCABULARY CROSSWORD ANSWER KEY - *Dicey's Song*

VOCABULARY WORKSHEET 1 - *Dicey's Song*

____ 1. Continued to stay; delayed; loitered
    A. Lingered   B. Harried   C. Cremated   D. Lurching

____ 2. Liable to fall or break down because of weakness
    A. Rickety   B. Contradict   C. Laden   D. Wary

____ 3. Showing resentment and ill humor
    A. Meandering   B. Reverberated   C. Sulky   D. Emanate

____ 4. Rolling, pitching or swaying suddenly
    A. Aureole   B. Convenient   C. Confer   D. Lurching

____ 5. To declare firmly and persistently
    A. Insisted   B. Meandering   C. Contradict   D. Sulky

____ 6. A travelling poet, singer or musician
    A. Wary   B. Minstrel   C. Convenient   D. Balmy

____ 7. A special quality that inspires allegiance and devotion
    A. Dumbfounded   B. Intrusion   C. Precisely   D. Charisma

____ 8. Inclination to move or act in a particular way
    A. Tendency   B. Confer   C. Rickety   D. Sulky

____ 9. Soothing; mild; pleasant
    A. Tendency   B. Balmy   C. Symmetrical   D. Diminished

____ 10. A radiance encircling the head or body; a halo
    A. Symmetrical   B. Aureole   C. Harried   D. Fluently

____ 11. To flow out; come forth; emit
    A. Enthusiasm   B. Interfere   C. Emanate   D. Harried

____ 12. Loaded; burdened
    A. Triumphantly   B. Wary   C. Laden   D. Lapel

____ 13. Models of the human body usually used in stores
    A. Confer   B. Laden   C. Precision   D. Mannikins

____ 14. Not sharp or certain; hazily
    A. Mannikins   B. Vaguely   C. Insisted   D. Wary

____ 15. Successfully; elated
    A. Dumbfounded   B. Triumphantly   C. Diminished   D. Cremated

____ 16. Cautious
    A. Wary   B. Balmy   C. Lapel   D. Tendency

____ 17. To be reflected as light or sound waves
    A. Intrusion   B. Optimistic   C. Reverberated   D. Tendency

____ 18. Burnt up; burned a dead body to ashes
    A. Insisted   B. Deceitfulness   C. Reverberated   D. Cremated

____ 19. Subdued; restrained from excess
    A. Fluently   B. Rickety   C. Chastened   D. Wary

____ 20. Expect the best outcome
    A. Optimistic   B. Balmy   C. Vaguely   D. Minuet

KEY: VOCABULARY WORKSHEET 1 - *Dicey's Song*

__A__ 1. Continued to stay; delayed; loitered
    A. Lingered   B. Harried   C. Cremated   D. Lurching

__A__ 2. Liable to fall or break down because of weakness
    A. Rickety   B. Contradict   C. Laden   D. Wary

__C__ 3. Showing resentment and ill humor
    A. Meandering   B. Reverberated   C. Sulky   D. Emanate

__D__ 4. Rolling, pitching or swaying suddenly
    A. Aureole   B. Convenient   C. Confer   D. Lurching

__A__ 5. To declare firmly and persistently
    A. Insisted   B. Meandering   C. Contradict   D. Sulky

__B__ 6. A travelling poet, singer or musician
    A. Wary   B. Minstrel   C. Convenient   D. Balmy

__D__ 7. A special quality that inspires allegiance and devotion
    A. Dumbfounded   B. Intrusion   C. Precisely   D. Charisma

__A__ 8. Inclination to move or act in a particular way
    A. Tendency   B. Confer   C. Rickety   D. Sulky

__B__ 9. Soothing; mild; pleasant
    A. Tendency   B. Balmy   C. Symmetrical   D. Diminished

__B__ 10. A radiance encircling the head or body; a halo
    A. Symmetrical   B. Aureole   C. Harried   D. Fluently

__C__ 11. To flow out; come forth; emit
    A. Enthusiasm   B. Interfere   C. Emanate   D. Harried

__C__ 12. Loaded; burdened
    A. Triumphantly   B. Wary   C. Laden   D. Lapel

__D__ 13. Models of the human body usually used in stores
    A. Confer   B. Laden   C. Precision   D. Mannikins

__B__ 14. Not sharp or certain; hazily
    A. Mannikins   B. Vaguely   C. Insisted   D. Wary

__B__ 15. Successfully; elated
    A. Dumbfounded   B. Triumphantly   C. Diminished   D. Cremated

__A__ 16. Cautious
    A. Wary   B. Balmy   C. Lapel   D. Tendency

__C__ 17. To be reflected as light or sound waves
    A. Intrusion   B. Optimistic   C. Reverberated   D. Tendency

__D__ 18. Burnt up; burned a dead body to ashes
    A. Insisted   B. Deceitfulness   C. Reverberated   D. Cremated

__C__ 19. Subdued; restrained from excess
    A. Fluently   B. Rickety   C. Chastened   D. Wary

__A__ 20. Expect the best outcome
    A. Optimistic   B. Balmy   C. Vaguely   D. Minuet

VOCABULARY WORKSHEET 2 - *Dicey's Song*

____ 1. AUREOLE   A. Coagulated; solidified or thickened

____ 2. ANTICIPATING   B. An aimless wandering; rambling

____ 3. PRECISELY   C. Models of the human body usually used in stores

____ 4. MANNIKINS   D. To declare firmly and persistently

____ 5. WARY   E. Meddle; hinder; prevent; intervene

____ 6. INTERFERE   F. Looking forward to or expecting

____ 7. TENDENCY   G. Exact correspondence of form on opposite sides of a dividing line

____ 8. PRECISION   H. Teasing; prank; naughty or troublesome act

____ 9. MEANDERING   I. To have a conference or talk

____ 10. CONGEALED   J. Particularly; exactly

____ 11. SYMMETRICAL   K. Inclination to move or act in a particular way

____ 12. SULKY   L. Exactness

____ 13. REVERBERATED   M. Showing resentment and ill humor

____ 14. MISCHIEF   N. Liable to fall or break down because of weakness

____ 15. LAPEL   O. To be reflected as light or sound waves

____ 16. INSISTED   P. A radiance encircling the head or body; a halo

____ 17. RICKETY   Q. Cautious

____ 18. OPTIMISTIC   R. Part of a jacket folded back from the neckline

____ 19. HARRIED   S. Tormented or worried; harassed

____ 20. CONFER   T. Expect the best outcome

KEY: VOCABULARY WORKSHEET 2 - *Dicey's Song*

__P__	1. AUREOLE	A. Coagulated; solidified or thickened
__F__	2. ANTICIPATING	B. An aimless wandering; rambling
__J__	3. PRECISELY	C. Models of the human body usually used in stores
__C__	4. MANNIKINS	D. To declare firmly and persistently
__Q__	5. WARY	E. Meddle; hinder; prevent; intervene
__E__	6. INTERFERE	F. Looking forward to or expecting
__K__	7. TENDENCY	G. Exact correspondence of form on opposite sides of a dividing line
__L__	8. PRECISION	H. Teasing; prank; naughty or troublesome act
__B__	9. MEANDERING	I. To have a conference or talk
__A__	10. CONGEALED	J. Particularly; exactly
__G__	11. SYMMETRICAL	K. Inclination to move or act in a particular way
__M__	12. SULKY	L. Exactness
__O__	13. REVERBERATED	M. Showing resentment and ill humor
__H__	14. MISCHIEF	N. Liable to fall or break down because of weakness
__R__	15. LAPEL	O. To be reflected as light or sound waves
__D__	16. INSISTED	P. A radiance encircling the head or body; a halo
__N__	17. RICKETY	Q. Cautious
__T__	18. OPTIMISTIC	R. Part of a jacket folded back from the neckline
__S__	19. HARRIED	S. Tormented or worried; harassed
__I__	20. CONFER	T. Expect the best outcome

VOCABULARY JUGGLE LETTER REVIEW GAME CLUES - *Dicey's Song*

SCRAMBLED	WORD	CLUE
TAGACINIPINT	ANTICIPATING	Looking forward to or expecting
EOAULER	AUREOLE	A radiance encircling the head or body; a halo
AYBLM	BALMY	Soothing; mild; pleasant
MHAISARC	CHARISMA	A special quality that inspires allegiance and devotion
DHATCEENS	CHASTENED	Subdued; restrained from excess
RCOFNE	CONFER	To have a conference or talk
ALCDOENGE	CONGEALED	Coagulated; solidified or thickened
IDRCTCAOTN	CONTRADICT	Oppose verbally; go against; assert the opposite
VECTENONIN	CONVENIENT	Easy to do, use, or get to
MATEDREC	CREMATED	Burnt up; burned a dead body to ashes
TSEIDUECLESNF	DECEITFULNESS	Dishonest action or trick; fraud or lie
HDMNIDSIIE	DIMINISHED	Made smaller; lessened; reduced
BOUFDEUMNDD	DUMBFOUNDED	Made speechless by shocking; amazed
ANETEMA	EMANATE	To flow out; come forth; emit
ETNHMASUSI	ENTHUSIASM	Intense or eager interest; passion
YTLEFULN	FLUENTLY	Write or speak easily, smoothly and expressively
RHIAEDR	HARRIED	Tormented or worried; harassed
TSDENSII	INSISTED	To declare firmly and persistently
FINEREET	INTERFERE	Meddle; hinder; prevent; intervene
ISUTNNRIO	INTRUSION	An invasion of privacy
DELAN	LADEN	Loaded; burdened
PALLE	LAPEL	Part of a jacket folded back from the neckline
INGLEDER	LINGERED	Continued to stay; delayed; loitered
CLINGURH	LURCHING	Rolling, pitching or swaying suddenly
KNAMINNI	MANNIKIN	Models of the human body usually used in stores
REDAMGENIN	MEANDERING	An aimless wandering; rambling
STINLREM	MINSTREL	A travelling poet, singer or musician
UNTIME	MINUET	A slow, stately dance or music for such a dance
SHEMIFIC	MISCHIEF	Teasing; prank; naughty or troublesome act
TOMIPCITIS	OPTIMISTIC	Expect the best outcome
RILYCEEPS	PRECISELY	Particularly; exactly
RESINCOPI	PRECISION	Exactness
REEVETBERDAR	REVERBERATED	To be reflected as light or sound waves
KIRTECY	RICKETY	Liable to fall or break down because of weakness
KULSY	SULKY	Showing resentment and ill humor
MYSLAMTIREC	SYMMETRICAL	Exact correspondence of form on opposite sides of a dividing line

www.ingramcontent.com/pod-product-compliance
Lightning Source LLC
LaVergne TN
LVHW081538060526
838200LV00048B/2137